SHAME AND THE ORIGINS OF SELF-ESTEEM

SHAME AND THE ORIGINS OF SELF-ESTEEM

A Jungian Approach

Mario Jacoby

Translated from the German in collaboration
with the author by Douglas Whitcher

London and New York

First published as *Scham-Angst und Selbstwertgefühl* by
Walter Verlag, Olten and Freiburg im Breisgau
© 1991 Walter Verlag

First published in English in 1994
by Routledge
11 New Fetter Lane, London EC4P 4EE

Simultaneously published in the USA and Canada
by Routledge
29 West 35th Street, New York, NY 10001

© 1994 Mario Jacoby

Typeset in Palatino by
Ponting–Green Publishing Services, Chesham, Bucks
Printed and bound in Great Britain by
Mackays of Chatham PLC, Chatham, Kent

British Library Cataloguing in Publication Data
A catalogue record for this book is available from
the British Library.

Library of Congress Cataloging in Publication Data
Jacoby, Mario.
[Scham-Angst und Selbstwertgefühl. English]
Shame and the origins of self-esteem: a Jungian
approach/Mario Jacoby: translated in collaboration
with the author by Douglas Whitcher.
p. cm.
Translation of: Scham-Angst und Selbstwertgefühl.
Includes bibliographical references and index.
1. Shame. 2. Self-esteem. 3. Psychotherapy.
4. Jung, C. G. (Carl Gustav), 1875–1961. I. Title.
BF575.S45J3313   1993
152.4–dc20   93–15067
CIP

ISBN 0–415–07526–2

CONTENTS

v

FOREWORD

It was none other than Georges Simenon, creator of the master detective Maigret, who brought home to me why I care to share with others my struggles with the "shadow" theme of shame. The realization came as I read the following:

> Everyone has a shadow side of which he is more or less ashamed. But when I see someone who resembles me, who shares the same symptoms, the same shame, and the same inner battles, then I say to myself, so I am not alone in this, I am no monster.

Simenon, a master psychologist and consummate author of suspense, thus helped me to see that a book about shame could even be a type of "psychotherapy" – not only for the author, as is usually the case, but perhaps for his readers as well. Now, I am skeptical of books that sell themselves to their readers with the alluring promise of making them happier, healthier, or wiser. Such achievements require real psychotherapy, which presupposes an encounter between two persons in the flesh. Even so, as I read the lines from Simenon I found myself thinking that perhaps individuals who are plagued with shame might find some liberation in hearing about others who suffer similar torments or take some consolation in knowing they are not alone. Certainly the wish to hide one's shame – and what one is ashamed of – is a universal human characteristic. Shame makes us want to sink through the floor, crawl into a hole and die. And then we really are alone.

I have long wondered why so little has been written on the subject of shame from the perspective of depth psychology. Hultberg expressed the same perplexity in 1988 in an essay tellingly entitled, "Shame: a Hidden Emotion." But with more research, I have discovered that a number of relevant publications have appeared in English, especially in the United States. These seem to me of great interest and worthy of mention in my ibliography (Kaufman 1989, Lynd 1961, Tomkins 1987, Lewis 1971, 1987a, 1987b, Miller 1985, Nathanson 1987, Izard 1977, Sidoli 1988, Wharton 1990, and others). A psychoanalytic monograph by Leon Wurmser titled *The*

Mask of Shame (1981) deserves special mention. It contains a plethora of profound and subtle insights into the unconscious dynamics of shame, and I strongly recommend it to anyone acquainted with psychoanalytical thought and terminology.

Still, to my knowledge, no book like the one I am now presenting currently exists. In writing it, I deliberately allowed myself to be led by my own subjective concerns – my "personal equation." For it is only by presenting what makes sense to me that I can speak to others in a convincing and credible way.

In the course of many years of practice as a psychotherapist and Jungian analyst, it has become clear to me that shame occupies a central place in our emotional experience. Thus I have often pondered the status of shame in the web of our psychosocial existence as a whole. I have observed various emotional nuances of shame in myself, my friends, and my clients. I suffered them myself – or vicariously and empathically suffered them with others – before I attempted to analyze them and fit them into a psychological framework. Naturally, I have also read and been inspired by the works of various specialists. In the present book, however, I intend to mention only those viewpoints that have been most meaningful to me personally and professionally.

Shame has many variations – an entire family of affects. These include not only feelings of inferiority and humiliation, but also shyness, inhibition, embarrassment, and so forth. It is not always obvious to the affected person that his different feelings are variations of the single emotion shame. Besides acute experiences of shame that the affected person identifies as such, there are shaming experiences that result in feelings of anxiety. I call this phenomenon "shame-anxiety," and mean by it the fear of being shamed, through one's own fault, one's own carelessness, adverse circumstances, or "coming on too strong" to others. These I believe are the variations of shame that one encounters most commonly, both in everyday life and in the practice of psychotherapy. That is why I have given shame-anxiety such a central place in my reflections.

Shame is intricately tied to one's social context. It revolves around the question of what respect I enjoy in others' eyes and what effect they have on my sense of worth as a person. The more I doubt my own self-worth, the more important the opinions of others become and the more sensitive I will be to the smallest hint of rejection. Thus, I have come to believe, a lack of self-confidence and self-esteem is the root cause of a susceptibility to shame. Any psychotherapy that would treat this susceptibility must begin by dealing with deficient feelings of self-worth.

Having arrived at this insight, I found that I must once again immerse myself in the complex question of self-esteem and its origins. Here my interest was drawn mainly to the field of modern infant research, which explicitly proves there is a strong link between our feelings of self-worth and the sense of worth we received from our childhood environments. The various forms of mother–child interaction, so vividly described in the literature on infant research, reminded me at every turn of the way my analysands and I deal with each other. From this, I have concluded that there is much to be learned from infant researchers about how to be in a therapeutic dialogue with people who suffer from disturbances of self-esteem. I would like to warmly thank Ms. Lotte Koehler, M.D., from Munich, for bringing these investigations to my attention – especially the work of Daniel Stern.

A word about my mode of presentation: as a Jungian analyst, I share with Jung the view that a science of the psyche can never sufficiently encompass the kaleidoscopic richness and complexity of the living soul. No psychological statement can ever do justice to such complexity. Naturally, I have made every effort to be as clear and concrete as possible. But, for the sake of psychological truth, I have all too often been forced to resort to such qualifying expressions as "could," "possibly," "perhaps," "often," and "it seems to me." For, many of the psychic configurations under discussion "could," "under other circumstances" and in "certain situations" be quite different – or differently construed. In addition, for the sake of readability, I have made the slightly old-fashioned decision not to report at every opportunity that I am thinking of, and desire to address, members of both sexes. For me, this is such a basic assumption that I do not find it necessary to thrust it before the reader's eye at every turn. Therefore, I hope I will not be accused of patriarchal prejudices for falling back on the pronouns "he" and "him" when referring to individuals generically.

It still remains for me to express my gratitude: to David Stonestreet, Publisher, from Routledge for encouraging the English version of this book; to Douglas Whitcher for his sincere and cooperative efforts in translating the text, and to Susan C. Roberts, who, with her sensitive editorial skills, put it into a clear and fluent English writing style. Further-more I want to address my sincere thanks to my analysands. Without the chance to learn from them in a reciprocal relationship, I would not have been able to write a book such as this one. I am especially grateful to those who gave me permission to describe vignettes from their therapy sessions – omitting all unnecessary data in order to protect their anonymity. Thanks are also due to my wife, Doris Jacoby-Guyot, for her inestimable help. In keeping with the spirit of the book, I will overcome my false shame in order to expose my intimate gratitude to her to the public eye.

So, bearing in mind the statement by Simenon, I hope by all of these means to have conveyed some understanding for how shame and shame-anxiety feel, with what they are linked, and how it is possible to work with them in therapy.

1

THE PHENOMENOLOGY OF SHAME AND SHAME-ANXIETY

THE DIFFERENCE BETWEEN SHAME AND GUILT

I will start with the assumption that both shame and guilt are generally human and archetypally given, but that it is not easy to distinguish between the two. They tend to appear in tandem, and so whether we identify an experience as shame or guilt becomes a question of inter-pretation. The following simple and familiar analogy may help us to distinguish between them. Feelings of guilt make me feel like a bad person because I have done something – or perhaps only thought about doing something – that I should not have done. But I may also feel bad if I fail to do something I should have done. Feelings of guilt have to do with ethical or moral principles called "should-laws" in philosophical ethics. It is revealing that in English the verb "should" is etymologically derived from the Middle English words *scholden, shulde, scholde, schulde*, and the Anglo-Saxon *scolde, sceolde*, meaning "I am obliged" (*Webster's* 1990). I thus remain in debt to some "should" whose fulfillment is generally held to be "good." This raises the complex issue of good and evil, an issue that brings conscience, or the intrapsychic authority responsible for making such distinctions, into play.

What is different about the way that shame manifests itself? At a certain intensity, shame has the power to make us feel completely worthless, degraded from head to foot, sometimes without our having done anything bad at all.

Once again, it is interesting to look into the etymology of the word. Etymological inquiries are usually of great psychological interest, for they reveal associations and connections that may assist in psychological inter-pretation. Etymologists have linked the modern English word "shame" with the Indo-Germanic root *kam/kem* meaning "to cover." The idea of covering oneself with a garment seems to have been implicit in the concept of shame for a long time (Wurmser 1981: 29) Later, the word "shame" was also used as an oblique reference to "private parts." Shame is also related

1

to disgrace, and is often used in literature – for example, by Shakespeare – to signify dishonor:

> But now mischance hath trod my title down
> And with dishonor laid me on the ground.

When one falls into disgrace, resulting in a loss of honor, one is degraded or demeaned, marked by a stigma or a stain. Jane Austen wrote of "a disgrace never to be wiped off," and Shelley of "the brand of infamy." It seems that the word shame has for some time been associated with experiences of discredit, humiliation, and injury.

As I mentioned, there is much overlap between shame and guilt. The guilt that one accumulates can put one in a shameful pit of disgrace and dishonor. One can also be ashamed of one's own badness. But what is unique about the feeling of shame is that it is not always a reaction to unethical behavior. One may be ashamed of having red hair, having a slight or tall build, or of being overly stout. Criminal deeds or negligence are not all that are capable of bringing on the contempt of society. Membership in a certain race or family, for instance, can also provoke a sense of inferiority. Thus shame results from the manner in which my entire being or self is valued – or, more precisely, devalued – not only by others but by myself.

Feelings of guilt appear when I cause another person injury or fail to live up to certain standards. But while I may feel ashamed of my unethical behavior, I can also be ashamed of my clumsiness or my weight. In any case, the feeling of shame always brings a loss of self-respect, whereas someone who feels guilty can hope to make amends.

On closer examination, we can see that often shame is felt as a deeper injury than guilt. Thus, feelings of guilt may serve as a defense against shame. For example, when someone is left by his lover, there is – besides the hurt associated with the withdrawal of love – a painful loss of self-esteem, the defeat of having been dumped. It may be less painful to search for what caused the relationship to break up than to imagine that one simply was not attractive or sexy enough. If a person does not simply escape the pain by blaming the other, he may prefer to think of the times that he was guilty of hurting, abandoning, and treating his lovers insensitively. Confessions of guilt also hold out the hope that mistakes will be rectified, all will be forgiven. But the feeling that one is personally unworthy of love cuts much deeper. This may be one reason that we tend to hear so much more about guilt than shame.

One can generally deny one's feelings of guilt through projective blaming of others, or defend against them with a compensatory posture of "standing up for my rights." However, there are also cases where shame serves as a defense against guilt – especially when guilt brings the possibility of punishment. In this case, one takes no responsibility for the specific deeds that trigger feelings of guilt but simply collapses into a remorseful swamp. This "posture of humility" takes the wind out of the opponent's sails, allowing him no response but pity. He who still desires to penalize the guilty party will only come to feel guilty himself if he persists in prosecuting a meek penitent. Such behavior is often played out unconsciously as a neurotic form of defense. However, it can also be a tactic employed very deliberately to disarm the prosecutor. A classic example from politics was Nasser's demonstrative remorse after Egypt lost the Six-Day War. The president lamented so long and abjectly about his guilt over this humiliating defeat that he eventually won the heart of his people again.

As I have mentioned, shame arises when our self-respect is doubted or under attack, whether from without or from within. Each of us has within ourselves a partially conscious image of the way we want to be seen – the so-called "ego-ideal." The higher this ego-ideal's demands are for perfection, the easier it will be to fall into feelings of inferiority and shame.

This touches on a problem that will be discussed at greater length later on. For now, let us summarize the matter as follows: in feelings of shame the demands of our ego-ideal make themselves painfully known, while in feelings of guilt the painful signals derive from our conscience – our so-called "superego." Feelings of shame are linked with the fantasy that I have been exposed to degradation, that I have been scorned by others and/or myself. The operative motif behind feelings of guilt, by contrast, is that I have done something that was not right.

In addition to these variations upon guilt and shame, there are psychic states in which the two emotions are in conflict with each other. For example, I think of a young man for whom all sexual activity was linked with guilt and sin. The problem manifested itself in his inability to reach orgasm during sexual intercourse and led him to avoid every possible form of intimate relationship. It was clear that his problem derived from his ambivalent bond to an extremely prudish mother. What brought him to psychotherapy, however, was the embarrassing symptom of blushing. Every time his fellow students began to speak about topics of a sexual nature, he was overcome with the fear of blushing. The analysis showed that this blushing concealed two contradictory, tormenting ideas. First, he was afraid that everyone he talked to would suspect he had a one-track mind occupied exclusively with sex, when actually, he was uncomfortable with the topic and inwardly disapproved of it the way his mother had. At the same time, he was afraid that his lack of masculine sexual prowess might be discovered. Then there was also his shame of blushing, which exposed his problem.

The following conflict was embodied in his symptom: according to his strict, religious mother, sexual acts and fantasies were sinful. If he violated her holy rule prohibiting sex, he sinned. If he obeyed her rule, he not only

3

repressed a portion of his instinctual energy, he also subjected himself to the shame of being less of a man than those around him.

Wurmser described a "guilt-shame dilemma" (1988: 288) in which one feels guilty for separating from one's parents and their partially internalized commandments – even though such a separation is crucial for the development of one's personality. In contrast to feelings we traditionally associate with the quest for autonomy and separation, one very often feels impotent, servile and exposed. These feelings of inferiority, of being unprepared for life, make one ashamed not only in front of others, but also before oneself. Wurmser saw guilt and shame as antithetical. Guilt is a response to strength and power, shame a response to weakness and impotence.

So in the example above, the man who suffered from fits of blushing was plagued by guilt whenever he began to feel inwardly strong and autonomous, whenever he began to disregard his mother's commandments. When such guilt feelings threatened the stability of his ego, he felt impotent once again and ashamed of his weakness.

This example brings us to the topic of emotional disturbances, which we will examine in more depth later on. Here I was concerned above all to present some thoughts on the distinction between feelings of shame and guilt.

ANXIETY AND SHAME

Anxiety also plays a large role in relation to shame, as can be seen when we speak of the fear of making fools of ourselves or of being caught in embarrassing or shameful situations. Though Freud did not propose an elaborate theory about shame, he was deeply interested in the psychological antecedents of guilt. In his view, guilt was a subspecies of moral anxiety, which is generated by the conscience, the "superego" (Freud 1923). Thus, anxiety is the genus – the master emotion – and guilt and shame are species derived from it. Guilt and shame are specific aspects of the many-sided phenomenon of anxiety.

What is anxiety? As far as we can tell, anxiety is an invention of nature whose aim is to protect life. We may not be able to determine whether or not a fly knows the emotion of anxiety, but if we chase a pesky housefly intending to kill it, it will adeptly maneuver an escape, behaving as if it knew fear. This may even move us to take pity; indeed, it is probably because of this projective empathy and its associated anxiety that some people cannot harm a flea. At least we can say that the fly has an inborn escape mechanism that corresponds to a pattern of response that in humans is linked with emotions of anxiety. Clearly anxiety is an emotion on the threshold between life and death. How often have those who are depressed and tired of life said that they would gladly put an end to their lives if only they were not so afraid to do it.

But human anxiety functions not only to promote our concrete, physical survival; it also appears when the ego's autonomy and need for control is threatened. Wild animals exhibit a behavior that we interpret as a response of anxiety (i.e., flight) but only in cases of physical threat. By contrast, we humans are capable of anticipating in imagination a wide variety of anxiety-provoking situations, since consciousness encompasses the dimension of time, forcing us to confront the uncertainty of the future. Long ago, Aristotle defined anxiety as "displeasure or unrest that arises from the idea of an impending, destructive misfortune or from a malady that brings displeasure" (quoted in Blaser and Poeldinger 1967: 12). Finally, anxiety is linked to the knowledge of our vulnerability to all kinds of unknowns and risks inherent in life. We have devised both individual and collective measures for safeguarding ourselves against such risk – including insurances against illness, old-age, unemployment, and other eventualities. Indeed, as the psychiatrist Kurt Schneider rightly observed:

> In view of the nature of human being, we are more in need of explanations for the fact that humans usually have no anxiety than we are for the fact that they sometimes do.
>
> (Schneider 1959: 28)

Indeed, one may well ask whether our culture – including both its light and dark sides – is based largely on the attempt to cope creatively with anxiety.

Feelings of shame can be qualitatively distinguished from those of anxiety, but they can also be seen as a particular form of anxiety. Then again, anxiety is always at work when we anticipate potential shame-producing situations. This is the case with examination-anxiety, stage-fright, fear of meetings with important persons, or certain forms of sexual anxiety. It is the anxiety associated with the prospect of getting into shameful situations in the near or distant future.

In the case of examination-anxiety, it is clear that failing an examination can have real consequences, adversely affecting one's career opportunities. But this is only one aspect. Fear of failing, of having to feel like a dumb jerk, contributes to our anxiety at least as much. Indeed, it is the fear of falling short of one's expectations of oneself, as well as the expectations of one's teacher, which most often lead to painful self-denigration.

But generally, examinations are part of conditions that must be fulfilled; we do not seek them out as occasions to expose ourselves. How much worse is the effect of stage fright, which strikes those who specifically desire to stand in the limelight. Discussion group leaders, givers of toasts, actors, musicians, lecturers all subject themselves to the expectation that they have something to offer that is worth the public's hearing or seeing. When they fail, their disgrace is compounded by the embarrassment of having their high opinion of themselves revealed for all to see.

By the same token, anxiety associated with impotence or frigidity is not nearly so painful because of the impairment of sexual enjoyment it causes as because of the shame it brings – that of being seen by one's partner as a failure, of not feeling like a complete man or woman.

Shame-anxiety thus revolves around the question: will I be able to fulfill the expectations of others or myself? Will I be successful, will I rate with a teacher, superior, or lover? Or will I take a beating and be shamefully put down?

Fear of shaming experiences can also lead to a reaction-formation consisting of excessive shyness or inhibition. Such a shy disposition often conceals a tendency to react with feelings of shame to occasions that could be in any way embarrassing. Whenever possible, such people avoid situations that are at all likely to cause shame. They feel it is better to keep silent than to risk making an inopportune comment, which could draw shameful attention to themselves. The famous Latin saying, "Si tacuisses, philosophus fuisses" ("If you had held your tongue, you would have remained a philosopher") expresses one justification of this form of defense. One is afraid of laying oneself open, standing out in the crowd, taking initiative, since these actions risk revealing one's ignorance and incurring a loss of self-respect and the esteem of others. At the same time, it may be just as uncomfortable to allow others to see that one is an inhibited person with nothing to say, someone whose light is under a bushel. In this respect, it can be shameful not to be noticed, to stand on the sidelines, to feel like an uninfluential nothing. Thus, a vicious circle gets started: fear of shameful vulnerability produces shyness, and feelings of shyness produce shame.

Psychological analysis reveals that beneath such anxieties and inhibitions there often lies a great need to be seen, loved, even admired. This need may be all the more acute for having met with frustration, rejection, or even ridicule when one was a child. Thus it may be associated with old psychic wounds as well as constantly exposed to new ones. At the same time, the ego may fear the strength of such needs, rejecting them, denying their very right to exist. This means that the ego takes over the role of the parental figures who first denigrated such needs. I am speaking here of the psychic suffering that today falls under the category of "narcissistic disorders." We will return to this topic in a later chapter.

HOW SHAME AFFECTS US

Up until now, we have been speaking of shame-anxiety, the fear of shaming situations, and the effects of shame. It is largely the anxiety-provoking expectation itself that brings on the shameful events of blushing, shaking, inhibited speech, impotence, etc. Anxieties narrow our freedom and impair our ability to attune ourselves to the requirements of a situation. They force us to keep observing ourselves all the time. For example, anxious expectation of impotence or frigidity distracts one's attention from one's partner. The resultant focus on oneself only further weakens sexual response. Likewise, anxiously monitoring oneself for foolish behavior, a faltering voice, or shaky hands blocks all spontaneity. One becomes awkward, inhibited, uncertain, and self-conscious. This may lead to an acute feeling of shame, a sense of sinking into a pit where everyone else – imagined or real – will see one's misery and laugh derisively.

The most traumatic experiences of shame usually occur in childhood and often leave a sense of emotional defeat that persists for the rest of one's life. For example, a 55-year-old man strongly disliked cherries because they reminded him of a shameful mishap that took place when he was ten years old and on a school field-trip. His mother, not thinking, had given him cherries to take with him, even though it is common knowledge that cherries, in combination with water from the drinking fountain, often cause diarrhea. On the way home in the train, this combination did its work rather suddenly. All the available toilets were occupied at the crucial moment, and so, with an awful burst, the accident came to pass as the boy stood right in the middle of the aisle of the train. In a flash he disappeared into a small water closet that had become vacant, and even after arriving at the final stop of the journey, could not be persuaded to open the door and come out, despite the teacher's insistent knocking, threatening, pleading, and promising. At length, he was extracted by a railroad worker armed with a key, and so there was no mercy for the boy, nor any way to avoid the feared running of the gauntlet. The entire class had waited for him, and as he emerged from the train, taunted him with cries of "Hosenscheisser" (dirty-pants, scardy-pants). When he arrived at home in his soiled, stinking pants, his mother immediately launched into an abusive diatribe, bewailing the terrible disgrace he had brought on the family, and then stuck him contemptuously in the bathtub. The next day he refused to go to school. Though the teacher forbade anyone to use the name "Hosenscheisser," whenever laughter broke out in the classroom, the boy immediately imagined that his classmates were entertaining themselves at his expense. Soon he went to a new school and was able to let down his guard. But in the back of his mind he feared his new schoolmates might be initiated into the secret of his disgrace by someone from his former, knowing class. For years to come, this man continued to regard himself as a "Hosenscheisser" – a crippling blow to his self-esteem. To this day the memory of the event is still linked with feelings of humiliating embarrassment.

A 45-year-old man cannot forget the following shame event that occurred when he was fourteen. As the son of "better people" he had been sent to a dancing school, but his clumsiness on the dance floor left him feeling rejected by his partners. At the school, there was a blonde girl who became the constant object of his thoughts and hopes. However, he lacked the courage to speak to her directly. So instead, after a great deal of hesitation, he sent her a passionate love letter. No sooner had he sent it off than he was overcome with shame, thinking about how she might roar with mocking laughter when she read it. The torment of such fantasies was nearly enough to douse the flame of his love. When, as expected, he received no answer, he avoided all contact with her, since all he could imagine was her scorn. This did not keep him from making periodic visits to her neighborhood in hopes of catching a glimpse of her. But when he saw her at a distance, laughing with friends, he was convinced that she was talking about his letter.

Both of the experiences I have just described involved areas in which a person is particularly susceptible to shame. The first case involving the anal zone is made the more acute by an upbringing that emphasizes cleanliness as an important measure of socialization. Mastery over the sphincter muscle indicates that the child has achieved a degree of autonomy; it is therefore a source of pride. Loss of control – especially in front of one's peers – means regression and unbearable humiliation. In full view, one has sunken not just to the level of an infant, but to that of a "dirty pig," a *Hosenscheisser*. The second case involved the first erotic feelings of an adolescent and the confession of his tender fantasies. As it happened, describing those feelings in a letter was too great a risk – in view of the boy's age. The erotic zone does finally provoke a literal unveiling – but it also produces a corresponding vulnerability.

The following is another inextinguishable memory of a shame experience, in this case involving an ethical issue. When he was thirteen years old, an analysand took a five-franc coin that belonged to his mother and had been lying around on a table. A young maid was held responsible for this theft, in spite of her protests that she was not guilty. The boy did not have the courage to confess his misdeed, and indeed denied it so stubbornly that the maid was fired. Thirty years later, the boy still recalled the reproachful yet imploring look she gave him when she was asked to leave. That look became the image of his guilt and shame for having been such a coward.

Such experiences of acute shame often leave painful traces. As the English poet John Keats wrote, "The unluckiest hours in our life are those in which we remember the past blushing – if we are immortal this is what hell must be like" (quoted in Hultberg 1988: 115).

Many of us know all too well those sleepless nights in which we are lashed with the memory of having made miserable fools of ourselves: how could we have behaved so impossibly and lost control so completely? How could we have talked on and on about things that are no one else's business? The threshold of shame is of course different with each individual. How quickly we feel ashamed, and how intensely, finally depends on the measure of tolerance we are able to summon for our own shadow sides. But here we are entering into the subject of coping with shame, which has been reserved for a later chapter.

THE SHAME OF BODILY NAKEDNESS

The biblical story of Paradise tells us that Adam and Eve were ashamed of each other as soon as they became aware of their nakedness. The fruit of the Tree of Knowledge opened their eyes to their nakedness, which has become an image for the original experience of shame. It was also shame that motivated Adam and Eve to sew fig leaves together in order to hide their nakedness.

This ancient image raises the question of whether it is an archetypal aspect of human nature to obscure the sex organs – called "shame-parts" in many languages – behind some sort of apron or loincloth. Is such a tendency for shame – paradoxically – natural for human beings, even innate? Or is it the result of upbringing and the morals of a prudish society?

The biologist J. Illies writes in his book *Zoology of the Human* (1971) that this motif of fig leaf as loincloth or veiling artifact is to be found among nearly all societies, even "primitive" ones. He sees this veiling as motivated by the feeling of shame. He also notes that, according to contemporary child psychology, young persons begin to display an impulse to hide their nakedness as a normal stage of maturation, in addition to the recognition of sex differences. He sees shame about direct physical gender-expression as commencing at the end of the Oedipal phase, or around five years of age. Though it may be possible to suppress this shame impulse by means of upbringing, it is generally true that nakedness no longer has to do with natural innocence by the time the five-year-old stage of consciousness has been reached. Lack of inhibition when looking at the nudity of adults of the opposite sex is, according to Illies, not a sign that a natural sex drive has been liberated, but rather a sign that it has been constrained by means of numbing or denial. In his words:

> If one were to put children by themselves on a solitary island in order to allow them to grow up according to the nature of their species, free from all repressive influences of society, they would reinvent the loincloth at the age of five because they are in such need of it, in order to grow in an emotionally healthy way, protected, into puberty, and so that they would be able to take it off when, in a personal encounter, they choose to give up the safely guarded possession of shame and to hand it over to the partner.
>
> (Illies 1971: 134)

Illies, who was a biologist and an ethologist, nevertheless sounds a bit

9

moralistic and unrealistic in this passage. The "personal encounter" in which one sets aside one's shame for the sake of intimacy, however desirable, is not usually attained so easily. The developmental processes that help to integrate one's sexuality and one's capacity for love are far more complicated and easily disturbed.

Clearly one wonders how it would be if children, uninfluenced by social conventions, were to grow up on a solitary island. It is a question about which aspects of behavior are inherent in the species, a question about the nature of the human being and its archetypal predispositions. However, the solitary island concept does not help us much in answering this question, for children can not grow up alone and free of influence but are by their very human nature very much in need of the care and guidance of adults. And this always makes social influences preprogrammed as well. It is our nature to be social animals that live and create their culture.

To what degree is the shame of nakedness an archetypal aspect of human nature? To what extent is it the product of social norms that are interiorized by the individual? To pursue these questions we will employ the method of "amplification" as recommended by Jung. Jung originally used this method of enriching and deepening a motif of the imagination as proof of his hypothesis of the archetypes of the collective unconscious. By discovering parallel motifs and symbolic meanings in diverse times and societies utterly free of mutual influence, he was able to find support for the possibility that he was dealing with generally human psychic predispositions. Thus, while this method may not provide a final answer to the question of whether a given facet of behavior is common to all members of the human species, it can nevertheless broaden our horizons for making interpretive links.

Thus I would like to pursue some ideas that throughout history have revolved around the theme of bodily nakedness and the human reproductive organs. Perhaps then we will come closer to a psychological understanding of the shame of nakedness.

It is well known that nudity often occurs in dreams. In the majority of such dreams, the dreamer experiences nudity as awkward and embarrassing – especially when the dream does not contain manifest sexual content, but rather concerns one's nakedness being exposed for all to see. It is noteworthy that collective notions about being naked and baring the genitals do not emphasize the sexual sphere primarily, at least not manifestly. However, the genitals are always accorded a special meaning – they become the basis of fantasies of what is extraordinary. Nowhere in cultural history do we find a purely matter-of-fact naturalness in regard to the sexual sphere. If such "naturalness" were the defining characteristic of uncivilized nature societies, we would have to conclude that there have never been any wild or "nature" peoples, primitive or uncivilized – at least within the last forty thousand years (Duerr 1988: 12). In other words, it does not seem completely "natural" for human beings to behave "naturally" in regard to their physical "nature."

To amplify this attitude toward bodily nakedness, I will draw upon various resources, including the *Dictionary of German Superstition* (*Handwörterbuch des Deutschen Aberglaubens*, Bächtold-Stäubli 1927), whose article under the heading "Nudity" is some fifty pages long. I have also consulted *The Concise Pauly Dictionary of Antiquity* (*Der Kleine Pauly. Lexikon der Antike* 1979) as well as the aforementioned *Nudity and Shame* (*Nacktheit und Scham*) by Duerr, which contributes a mountain of information. Of course I have the space here to refer to only a few examples.

In many societies, naked exposure was used to punish adulterers. In Russia, peasants bound adulterous women naked to plows that tilled the soil. As Bächtold-Stäubli wrote:

> Punishment of adultery with shaming exposure of the "aidoia" is based on an ancient tradition of humiliating and disgracing the opponent through exposure.
>
> (Bächtold-Stäubli 1927)

That the author himself feels the shame involved here is indicated by his use of an unfamiliar Greek word, *aidoia*, for the sex organs. Literally translated, this word means "shame-parts," (from *aidos*: shame). In Babylon and Egypt, many sculptures portrayed the enemy naked. The ancient Jews considered it a heinous crime to bare one's "shame" before Yahweh, and the same theme clearly comes through in the life of Mohammed. (It is still forbidden to enter a synagogue without covering one's head. By the same token, the God of the Christians – especially the Catholics – does not care to see indecently clothed tourists in His churches, for example, wearing short pants or short-sleeved shirts.) While in cult processions nudity can be a sign of humility, in Christian culture complete nudity on pilgrimages was replaced early on by naked feet and unbound hair.

In antiquity, by contrast, the spring ceremonies included a good bit of erotic, orgiastic activity in honor of the gods. Certain gods in ancient Greece were responsible for the erotic sphere of life – one thinks of Aphrodite, Dionysus, Hermes, and Priapus, the last being identified with and portrayed by the phallus. But in Homeric times there was clearly shame of nakedness – even athletes wore a covering for their exercises. Later, in post-Homeric times, men and women who bathed together wore a special kind of bathing suit. Then again, to judge from evidence from Sparta and Crete, nudity continued in archaic times among men in sports. Such nakedness clearly expressed a pride and joy in one's own body. Devotional contemplation of the body in action contributed vitally to the blossoming of Greek art – one thinks, for example, of Praxiteles in the fifth century before Christ. But this was only true of the masculine body. When the female body was portrayed, it was usually for cultic reasons.

Concerning the famous, shame-free, naked Greek athletes doing their exercises in the "gymnasium" (from the Greek *gymnos*: naked), Duerr concluded that even there, feelings of shame followed certain rules. It was highly improper to allow the glans of the penis to be seen; it had to be kept covered by the foreskin at all times. Men doing athletic exercises drew the foreskin over the glans and tied it with a string. To the Greeks, a short foreskin was a clear sign of a dissipated sexual life. Thus when Jews began to appear in the exercises, their circumcized penises became a source of deep embarrassment. As a result, a provision was made that Jews would be allowed to take part in the Olympic games of Tyros only if they had their foreskins replaced. There were special operations for this, as the physician Galen reported (Duerr 1988: 19). One must also remember that women were forbidden to look at the naked athletes; that the Etruscans seem to have allowed this caused some scandal (Duerr 1988: 18). As far as the Athenians were concerned, the so-called "nudity" of the young Spartan girls was continuously scandalous. In reality, they were not at all naked while exercising, but wore a short *chiton* (a kind of skirt) which still outraged the athletes because it did not cover their thighs and both of their breasts. An exception seems to have been the "ritual nudity" of the Arktoi, the young she-bears. These were small girls as well as some older girls on the verge of adulthood who let their chitons fall to the floor during a maturation ritual. However, nothing indicates that this baring took place in the presence of men (Duerr 1988: 21). Duerr came to the conclusion that "classical Greece – to say nothing of Homeric times – was no Arcadia of shame-free masculine nakedness, as has been idealistically maintained time and again since the Renaissance" (Duerr 1988: 19). As for the Romans, they found athletic nudity unequivocably offensive. According to Plutarch, Romulus seems to have ordered the death penalty for anyone appearing naked in public.

The bounds of shame were not necessarily any more relaxed in the naked bathing customs of Japan in the last century or in the Finnish sauna, according to Duerr. In these and other such situations, one was expected to guard against the "indiscreet glance," keeping one's eyes averted from the sexual organs of other bathers. Similar practices have been reported among tribes of so-called "nature societies," whose social life is conducted in complete nakedness. Among the Kwoma, who go without clothes in the Peilungua mountains north of Depik, even small boys were punished if they were caught looking at a woman's or girl's genitals. The tribe's name for *vulva* corresponds exactly to the English expression "private parts." If a man looked at it directly, it was assumed he was making a seduction attempt and he was punished by the relatives of the woman in question (Duerr 1988: 135).

These few examples confirm the hypothesis that the practice of nudity hardly implies an absence of shame. In some ancient dreambooks, nudity in dreams is seen as a sign of a threat, possibly even the threat of death. According to an Indian teaching, dreaming that one is suddenly without clothes, so that one's "shame" is seen by everyone, foretells a revelation of one's secret that will end in disgrace and defeat. According to Persian and Egyptian teachings, a woman who dreams of undressing completely will betray her husband and be apprehended (Bächtold-Stäubli 1927).

Wickler has described another idea that revolves around the male organ (1973: 248). This ethologist noticed that some of the higher apes attempt to impress their foes by aggressively displaying the penis and scrotum. This is meant as a demonstration of their position in the hierarchy and as a gesture of threat. Among the baboons, for example, some male members serve as watchers. While the group eats, the watchers sit at the outer edge with their legs spread apart, their backs turned toward the group. If members of another group approach, the watcher displays his erect penis with the intention of scaring off the intruder and protecting his own group. Wickler saw this behavior as related to phallic figures discovered in Greece and Indonesia that not only symbolized fertility but also served as guardians against evil spirits.

The "military nudity," discovered mainly in Sparta but also in Corinth and even to some extent among the armies of Alexander the Great, clearly had a similar meaning. Soldiers from other regions also fought naked, or at least naked from the waist down. According to Duerr, a certain ancient horseman figure gives rise to the belief that soldiers of antiquity sometimes relied on the baring of the penis to threaten their enemies.

For Duerr, those who engaged in "military nudity" were persons who had been cast out and therefore were beyond the pale of civilization. They were the wild ones, made impure by having spilled blood. But one could just as well interpret this phenomenon as a phallic display pattern. In the imagination, the penis may be endowed with magical omnipotence such that the sight of it instills fear in the enemy. Here we might mention the practice of some archaic peoples who, though they may not have put their naked male organs on display, covered them with codpieces to make them appear extra large, obvious, and threatening. In the same spirit, European soldiers used to carry their swords – the proud attribute of manly military courage – like erect penises.

In our own times, protesters sometimes appear naked in order to stimulate public outrage. Even in a city as conventional as Zurich, young demonstrators ran stark naked down the famous Bahnhofstrasse a few years ago. Above all, it is the naked posterior that is presented as a gesture of contempt – a gesture obviously related to various verbal epithets concerning the anal zone or ass.

In summary, I will say that throughout human culture, nudity has taken on various unusual meanings that can be mutually contradictory. Nakedness is related on the one hand to the humiliation of being stripped, but on the other to the will to power and dominance. In Judaeo-Christian culture, stripping before God is a shameless sin. However, as a matter of penance, appearing "naked and stripped before God" can be a sign of profound humility. Cultic nudity was a requirement in ancient rites of initiation, which usually had the meaning of a symbolic rebirth. It was also important to the Greek gods of the mystery cults that participants be naked, just as it was believed that the Indian god Shiva desired that dances to him be performed without clothing (Bächtold-Stäubli 1927).

Bodily nakedness is not exclusively associated with sexuality and the partial drives of voyeurism or exhibitionism – at least not on the manifest level. However, it is clear that the potential for sexual attraction in physical nakedness is one of the most important causes of shame. For any society, it is important to keep unbridled instinctuality in check and to redirect sexuality into civilized channels. At the same time, the bounds of shame are determined by various morals and customs that express collective attitudes toward sexuality. To overstep these boundaries is shameless and brings disgrace.

Morals and customs regulating sexual behavior are often linked with the cultic domain. Hence the interpretation that the permission of the deity needs to be obtained before one indulges animalistic lust. But such an interpretation is unsatisfying, since sexual union can also be experienced as a mystery, for example as a cosmic marriage of opposites. An example would be the ancient Oriental institution of the "sacred prostitute" with whom a stranger could spend a night in the temple in order to celebrate the "sacred marriage" (Qualls-Corbett 1988). The sacred prostitute was distinguished from the profane prostitute, who offered her body for remuneration and was an object of disgrace and discrimination at all levels of society (Qualls-Corbett 1988: 37ff.; Duerr 1988: 300). In the Judaeo-Christian tradition, a marriage had to be blessed before God in order for sexuality to be lived in a permissible fashion rather than as a "shameful sin." In Catholicism it must even be raised to the level of a sacrament. Among the Greeks, the gods themselves inspired love and sexuality. However, each god ruled within a sphere that was only one of many, and that could thus come into conflict with others. No single god was powerful beyond all bounds. Themis, the goddess of good morals, had her say as well.

There probably does exist in all humans an archetypal threshold whose transgression provokes a reaction of shame. The manner in which this threshold of shame functions – the sanctions to which it is linked, whether it is rigid or flexible, lower or higher – is in each case a matter of collective and individual attitudes and the tolerance of the times. For example, nudist culture is more or less tolerated today in the West. But that does not mean that in some places nudists are not looked at askance; nudists have even at times been the victims of physical attack. The original nudists were sun-worshipers, members of a "back to nature" cult. They were of the view "that raw sensual drives could be killed off by contemplating pure and innocent nakedness" (Duerr 1988: 150). Of course, the fact that nudists cultivated strict discipline in order to avoid any possible sexual excitation (Duerr 1988: 150), raises the question of whether they were really practicing "natural" ways of living. Today, attitudes toward such matters have loosened somewhat. The fearful, uptight division between nakedness and eroticism is becoming much rarer. Thus certain nude beaches have become hotbeds for persons with exhibitionistic or voyeuristic tendencies.

But nudity in the light of the day and heat of the sun is usually far less erotic than, for example, a striptease show with the lights turned low. The latter is not only a display of physicality, but a tantalizingly gradual peeling away of the clothing. It is thus much more about playing with the threshold of shame and its violation, and thereby produces a certain pleasurable tingle.

I hope these comments have sufficed to establish the association of the archetypal feeling of shame with the unveiling of physical nakedness. Of course, I feel it is important to stress that when I speak of an archetypal predisposition, I am not implying any determinism of an individual's conscious attitudes and ways of behaving. On the contrary, it is the personal confrontation with archetypal predispositions – and social givens as well – that constitutes the essence of the maturation and individuation process.

2

THE PSYCHOLOGICAL
MEANING OF SHAME

SHAME IN THE BIBLICAL PARADISE NARRATIVE

What is archetypal about the emotion of shame? In the last chapter, we found that shame can be seen as an innate affect (Izard 1977), which suggests that it is irreplaceable in the economy of the psyche. Over the ages, archetypal experiences and behaviors have crystallized in the form of mythical ideas. Myths provide an array of expressive possibilities that in their symbolism, sensuality, and imagery move us to a process of endless contemplation and interpretation. As the Indologist Heinrich Zimmer observed:

> Those who wish to discuss a symbol say more with their explanations about their own limits and biases – especially if they are caught up in its meaning – than they do about the symbol's depths.
>
> (Zimmer 1938: 11)

Nevertheless, an exploration of myth broadens our understanding and stimulates new psychological insights. In our own cultural sphere, the most important myth dealing with the theme of shame – and guilt – is the biblical Paradise narrative (Gen. 3:1–24). The report derives from the so-called "Jahwist" and can be dated approximately to the tenth or ninth century before Christ, or the Solomonic Enlightenment, a time of crisis for many ancient sacred traditions. In the paradise narrative, feelings of both shame and guilt are depicted as originating in an act of disobedience to God, who had strictly forbidden humans to eat from the Tree of Knowledge. Before this violation, the biblical text claims, "And they were both naked, the man and his wife, and were not ashamed." But after they tasted of the tree of knowledge, their eyes were opened "and they knew that they were naked; and they sewed fig leaves together, and made themselves aprons" (Gen. 3:7). As God was walking in the cool of the day, they hid themselves so that He had to call out to Adam, "Where art thou?" Adam hid because he had realized that he was naked. "I was afraid, because I was naked; and I hid myself." "Who told thee that thou wast naked?" was

16

God's reply. Adam's awareness of his nakedness is what exposed his violation of God's commandment; it was proof that he had eaten from the Tree of Knowledge. From that moment on, he knew about good and evil, and therefore forfeited the experience of paradisal "unitary reality" (Neumann 1988).

It should be noted that the motif of a loss of a paradisal, unitary reality is not unique to this Jewish creation story, later adopted by Christianity. Many African myths also tell of how a mistake or violation of a commandment results in a momentous loss. The Greeks also saw their own Golden Age as having been lost due to human fault. Hubris, which literally means "pride" or "presumption," is the word they used to describe human behavior that oversteps limits set by a divine order of being. We find a classical example of hubris in the myth of Prometheus's theft of fire. Here humans steal something that belongs to the gods; they take divine privilege into their own hands. The biblical God suggests Adam has committed this same transgression when He says, "Behold, the man is become as one of us, to know good and evil" (Gen. 3:22; see also Jacoby 1985).

The capacity to distinguish between the opposites is at the very root of human consciousness – indeed, it virtually defines human nature. Paradoxically, it is both an offense against God's creation and an opportunity given by God. According to Herder, the human being is a creature set free from nature. Unlike other creatures, humans are not completely bound to nature by means of their instinctual endowment. They can and must pit themselves against nature; that is the source of their presumption, forlornness, and disorientation. Adolf Portmann described human nature as "openness to the world" and "freedom of choice," qualities that distinguish humans from animals, which are "environmentally-embedded" and "instinct-secured" (Portmann 1958).

Openness to the world and free will imply a certain loss of instinctive confidence. Still, human beings cannot divorce themselves entirely from their biological and instinctual foundations, however rudimentary these may be. One of the most difficult tensions that human beings have to cope with as a species comes from simultaneously belonging to nature and reflecting consciously on it. It is no wonder that we experience consciousness as a double-edged sword, even as "original sin."

The doctrine of original sin as it is generally understood today can be traced to Augustine, who lived from AD 354 to 430. It was he, above all others, who reduced this original guilt to sexuality. In this, he was clearly influenced by the contemporaneous movements of Neoplatonism and Gnosticism, which posited that the spirit had to be liberated from its imprisonment in corporality and instinctuality. It is well known that after his conversion to Christianity Augustine, who had led an active erotic life in his youth, wanted to drive out the devil of sex with the Beelzebub of intolerance. For him, the Fall entailed, above all, a transformation of sexuality – the beginning of all "lust" or "concupiscence." On the other hand, Augustine wanted to show that sexual relations without carnal desire are possible, and this formed the basis for his elaborate theory of "marriage in Paradise" (Grimm 1972). Since Augustine, the Fall has been interpreted primarily as a matter of sexuality, although this view is not necessarily grounded in the biblical text. I believe Augustine has caused a great deal of damage with his theory of "marriage in Paradise." This doctrine, I believe, has led to an unrealistic conception of sexuality and a sense that sexual lust is something that can be curbed at will. Augustine's theory was seminal in the development of a sexual ethic hostile not only to instinct but also to women.

In my book *The Longing for Paradise*, (1985) I reflected on several aspects of the Paradise narrative from a psychological point of view. In that account, I was especially interested in the idea of original sin in relation to the psychogenesis of conscience and guilt. But I did not deal with the feelings of shame also mentioned in the story, and I would like to fill that gap now.

The feeling of shame emerged for the first time after Adam and Eve's "eyes were opened." Having tasted the fruit of knowledge, they realized that they were naked. Obviously, they had been naked before, but this was no cause for concern – or shame – since it was nothing out of the ordinary. Reactions of shame are sparked off by awareness.

The following observation is also of psychological interest: the feelings of shame were so unbearable that "the man and his wife" found it necessary to do something. The solution lay in crafting protective loin-cloths for themselves out of fig leaves. This was a creative act, motivated by shame, for the sake of civilization. Nevertheless, the question remains as to why the first humans had to be ashamed in front of each other and even in front of God once they became conscious of their nakedness. In the story, this is related matter-of-factly, as if it required no further explanation. As I have said, it may simply be that the shame of completely exposing oneself has an archetypal foundation. It seems to be a trait of the species, a primal symptom of humanity's fall from unity with nature. In this respect, it does make sense to speak of a Fall. Humans no longer enjoy the condition of acting naturally in relation to what is natural. And this is precisely what tips God off to the fact that the "sin" of consciousness has taken place.

Of course it would not be wrong to interpret the tasting of the fruit of knowledge as the first act of love. This somewhat prevalent view builds on the Old Testament association of sexual relations and knowledge. In numerous places one reads that Abraham, Isaac, Jacob, and other patriarchs "knew" their wives in the night, after which the women bore sons. Even today, we describe the first act of love as a loss of innocence.

In the Sumerian-Babylonian epic of Gilgamesh, the link between the growth of human consciousness and the sexual encounter is even more explicit than in the Paradise narrative. In it, Enkidu, a natural man who lives with the animals and understands their speech, is seduced into an act of love by a "Hierodule," a sacred prostitute. Performing this act alienates him from his original nature and deprives him of his understanding of the language of the animals. Here, the symbolism suggests that the human sex-act is not merely an "instinctual-animalistic" phenomenon, but includes a rich realm of subjective experience – ideas, fantasies, and thoughts.

Being human entails a recognition that the shame of physical nakedness also has a psychic and therefore a symbolic significance. The first people's realization that they were naked coincided with a first perception of their own body image or body pattern. Distinctions were thus drawn; along with the knowledge of good and evil, there arose the capacity to distinguish I from Thou, subject from object. Adam and Eve are no longer one; they become conscious that they are two different persons – his naked body and her naked body. Each has a need to hide his nakedness from the other – a need that leads to mutual differentiation and also to the process of individualization.

At the same time, Adam realizes that God is a power separate from himself. From this power he hears the call, "Adam, where art thou?" Psychologically, this is to say that a differentiation has occurred between a consciousness centered in the ego and a consciousness of "something larger within us." (Jung called this greater something the "Self" and saw it as the imperceptible center of the entire personality, conscious and unconscious. The Self cannot be distinguished from the various god-images of the psyche.)

The myth of Paradise portrays an essential paradox in the growth of human consciousness. From the perspective of God, the human has become "like one of us, knowing good and evil." This knowledge produces a degree of "god-likeness" within the human. From the human perspective, however, it is this very growth of consciousness that brings man to recognize his limitations, his "nakedness" before God. Growth of consciousness creates a fear of God, a fear of being subjugated to something larger and more powerful. "I was afraid, because I was naked."

Humility and consciousness of the limits of the ego are some of the most difficult and important achievements along the path of psychic development. The ego must not identify with the supraordinate Self, for this would mean a fall into illusory or delusory fantasies of grandiosity, indeed into mental illness. At best, the ego stands in relationship with that which is greater in us, the Self, drawing a certain confidence from it: "self-confidence" in the deepest sense. We will return to this idea later on.

The growth of consciousness, symbolized by the eating of the fruit of knowledge, leads to a loss of paradisal unitary reality. No longer does one enjoy blissful ignorance of the painful conflicts caused by the polarization of inner and outer, subject and object, ego and Self (Neumann 1988). Consciousness centered in the ego is based on the differentiation of these opposites and the suffering of their polarity.

There are many positions one can take in regard to the proverbial fig leaf. Indeed, plenty of hypocrisy has hidden behind its protective veil. And yet, staying with the symbolism of the myth of Paradise, the fig leaf seems to be connected to the first creative act of human beings: "They sewed fig leaves together and made themselves aprons." The feeling of shame motivated them to find a remedy for their nakedness; it led to an invention. Adam and Eve attempted to cope with shame rather than remaining helplessly subject to it. In the process, they discovered the specifically human capacity for altering what is given by nature. Like anxiety, shame can be seen as a driving force of civilization.

THE BASIC FUNCTION OF SHAME

Why are we ashamed? This is a question of major psychological import. In the case of nakedness, for example, just what is it that we feel we have to hide from each other? Our physical make-up is basically the same as that of everyone else's of our gender. And almost all of us are more or less ashamed to let our naked bodies be seen. By exposing ourselves we even run the risk of being charged with "offending public decency."[1] Still, naked bodies do not by themselves harbor any great mystery.

"Don't act so modest; I know what boys and girls look like," one hears adolescents say in an attempt to overcome their shame about investigating each other's bodies. Bodily evacuations, urination, and defecation are natural and common to all, and yet they take place in a "closet" (or "closed" place) – as if there were something degrading about such animal necessities. Hence expressions such as, "Now I have to go find that little place where the Emperor (or the Pope) also kneels down." Sexual activities as well generally take place in an enclosed, private area, because sex partners would feel disturbed if they were observed during their love-play. (Such disturbances often take place in dreams, however; often the observer appears in the guise of father or mother!)

It seems logical to interpret such shame reactions as defenses against exhibitionistic or voyeuristic tendencies, tendencies that undoubtedly would lose some of their fervent appeal if they were not bound up with a collective taboo. Izard expressed the view that from a biological, evolutionary perspective, shame is probably the fundamental motive that leads people to seek privacy for sexual relations. Adherence to rules protecting privacy has long been in the interest of social order and harmony. In many ways, shame continues today to serve these functions in contemporary society (Izard 1977: 400).

Shame in its many forms – each with its particular pain and occasional neurotic side-effect – occupies an important place in our psychic and social economy. We "set ourselves apart" and keep to ourselves, as our language so clearly states. "It's nobody's business" what goes on in my fantasy, thoughts, and intimate life. Shame guards this inner sanctum and advises me about what I ought to show and share of myself, and what I would rather keep to myself. From a global perspective, all persons may have been created equal, biologically, psychologically, that is archetypally. And yet each individual safeguards his or her personal secrets in a private realm of shame, with its unique threshold that may be higher or lower, more rigid or flexible, than his neighbor's.

Shame reinforces interpersonal distinctness and a sense of one's own individual identity. On the other hand, an excessive tendency toward reactions of shame may lead to disturbances of contact and social isolation. At the same time, shame acts as a powerful inducement toward social adaptation, as it is often triggered by awkward self-consciousness and fear of criticism. Shame's function is thus highly complex, serving the interests of both individuality and conformity.

Must this contradiction lead to conflicts within the individual? First, let us say that it is society that demands a particular degree of discretion from each individual, which is why shame is an important factor in the socialization of children. Society decides what befits the individual, what is proper according to social mores. It limits displays of bodily nakedness, tolerates sexual activity only in private, and punishes offenses against public decency. Public confessions of private feelings likewise often cause embarrassing reactions, or awkward silences. Thus feelings of shame seem to safeguard certain agreed-upon boundaries that one violates only at the risk of social sanctions and personal exposure. Society expects a certain degree of privacy, and shame here stands in the service of social conformity. At whatever degree of intensity, individual wishes and demands come into conflict with society's expectations.

Conflicts within the shame experience itself first arise in the individual when the two functions of shame – "guardian" of individualization and of social adaptation – are experienced as contradictory. In this respect, Aristotle made an important distinction between the shame one feels about things that are offensive to "general opinion" and about things that are offensive to "the pure truth" (Lynd 1961: 239). In the same way, Hultberg refers to a distinction drawn by members of a tribe in New Guinea between "skin shame" and "deep shame" (1988: 118). For example, to be observed urinating or having sexual intercourse generates a feeling of skin shame. But to insult spirits of the ancestors provokes a reaction of deep shame. In the first case, shame is an emotional response to the violation of social norms. The second form of shame comes into play with the violation of an inner value system associated with the ego ideal.

These opposing functions can lead to conflicts within one's sense of shame itself. For example, I may be too ashamed to express my dissenting opinion in a group for fear of being laughed at, rejected, or not taken seriously. But as soon as I arrive home, I am ready to "kill myself" for shame for having been such a coward, so incapable of standing up for myself. I lose self-respect because I did not stand up for what is true for me – indeed, I may have even denied it. Such conflicts of shame are frequent. On the one hand, shame is the deputy of an unwritten, partially internalized moral and social code, while on the other it is the defender of inner sincerity, the lattice of our deepest convictions.

One of the most compelling passages in the New Testament addresses this conflict: Peter's thrice-repeated denial that he was a disciple of Jesus to avoid being ashamed before the bystanders. After the cock crowed (and he became conscious of what he was doing), Peter remembered the words of Jesus, went away and wept bitterly, feeling ashamed about his cowardice that Jesus had prophesied (Matt. 26). J.S. Bach has composed some of the most moving music in the St John and St Matthew Passions for this passage of the liturgy. Through it, we come to share in Peter's bitter remorse and shameful tears.

Hultberg perceptively observes that the two forms of shame are very different by nature and actually have opposing functions (1988: 118). As I have said, one form serves social adaptation, the other personal integrity; one guarantees adherence to societal norms, the other protects the individual from the collective. Between the two lies a potential for conflict that is inherent in the nature of the human species.

Shame resides on the borderline between self and other. It plays a critical role in the mediation of interpersonal closeness and distance, sensitively gauging my feelings about how close I can and want to let someone come.

Of course, trust enters into the equation as well. I must trust that the others will respect my self-esteem and integrity if I decide not to conceal from them "the naked truth" of who I really am. Fear of being hurt by an intimate encounter has to do with the fear of being exposed, ridiculed, and shamed – whether in an obvious or a subtle way. Interpersonal contact requires that one develop a high degree of sensitivity to the "right" balance of closeness and distance – a job in which the feeling of shame can be of substantial help. How often have I been tormented by the shame of having revealed too much about myself to someone whom I later decided had not earned my trust?

The familiar, if not banal, advice to not trust "just anybody" contains a deep truth, if only because trust is extremely complex and easily disturbed. Uncritical trust may not only be naive, but also self-destructive, especially when there may be open or hidden rivalry requiring one to stay on guard. To survive, it is necessary to develop a keen sense for who one can and cannot trust.

The capacity to realistically apportion trust and mistrust is usually bound up with one's childhood story, which determines the degree of differentiation possible for each individual. The childhood story can also be the cause of various disturbances, a topic that I will be discussing at greater length when I deal with the shame-complexes and their treatment in therapy. The essential element is always trust in one's own powers and inner values – or in a nutshell, "self-confidence." The less self-confidence and self-esteem one has, the greater the likelihood that one will fall victim to intense shame and fear of shame. Therefore the next chapter will be devoted to an in-depth exploration of the psychological basis of self-esteem.

3

THE FEELING OF
SELF-ESTEEM

HUMAN DIGNITY

Today, everyone seems to know what self-esteem is. But when we stop to think about what the feeling of self-esteem is made of and how it comes about, we see what a complex matter it really is. A great deal has been written on the topic as it relates to psychoanalysis, especially as a part of the sweeping interest in narcissism; indeed, from a psychoanalytic perspective, disturbances of self-esteem belong to the realm of narcissistic disorders. Recently, there has also been a dramatic rise in the number of studies dealing with the complex topic of the "self." I cannot embark on a detailed discussion of the various views that have been argued here, preferring to restrict myself to a few points directly relevant to our topic.

Self-esteem refers to the worth or dignity that one ascribes to oneself. In German, the word *Selbswertgefühl* makes this clear: it is a feeling (*Gefühl*) of worth (*Wert*) that we have of our selves (*Selbst*). The word "esteem," derived from the Latin word *aestimare*, denotes an estimation that I make of my own value. This is relevant in connection with the problem of shame-anxiety, since one could describe shame as a "guardian" of dignity. Shame-anxiety puts us on guard against "undignified" behavior, sensitizing us to whether or not a given event will be experienced as "degrading."

The word "dignity" sounds a bit old-fashioned, even pompous to us today. We think of "dignitaries" occupying exalted positions or "reverend fathers" comporting themselves with "dignity." To say that "it is beneath my dignity" to get mixed up with someone or something can easily make one sound arrogant.

In the past, one's sense of one's own worth and dignity was often linked to one's social standing. With the coming of the Enlightenment and the aesthetic and moral idealism of Kant and Schiller, the notion of an individual's self-worth was transformed and internalized. It took on the meaning of "self-esteem, the feeling of integrity, self-respect, that is, the feeling and consciousness of what one is responsible for, what one must do, or may not do, if one does not wish to lessen or forfeit one's dignity as

24

a person" (*Würde*, in Grimm and Grimm 1960). Goethe wrote the following on ethical worth:

> Here [in my breast] I feel something that moves, that says to me, "Rameau, don't do it." There must be a certain dignity deeply and irradicably embedded in human nature.
>
> (Goethe 1873)

In such writings, the concept of dignity is linked to an ethic of personal conduct. The failure to heed one's conscience results in a sense of shame, because one feels one's personal self-worth has been lessened.

The present century, with its concentration camps and totalitarian governments, provides abundant examples of how psychic, physical, and sexual rape can traumatize a victim's sense of personal dignity so severely that shame prohibits him from even speaking about it. Less harmful injuries to our personal dignity are the stuff of daily life, and often give rise to painful feelings of shame, rejection, degradation, and insult. Some people are particularly sensitive or vulnerable to such injuries.

On the one hand, the sense of personal dignity is necessary to our existence. On the other, it is considered tactless or tacky to emphasize one's dignity too much – or even to speak favorably of it. One is then seen as a braggart or boaster, and meets with social disfavor. It is undignified – showing off – to put one's dignity on display.

Our personal dignity consists not only of our own self-worth but our sense of the worth of everything we feel belongs to us – marriage partner, family, clan, perhaps even religion and nation. Maintaining this dignity is a function that, from an archetypal perspective, holds a central position in the economy of the psyche. However, the definition of what is dignified varies widely from one person to another, as does the place where shame marks the boundary to indignity. These variations depend on hierarchies of values created by societies, families, and individuals. For centuries, we in the Occident were proud of our rationality, that faculty that gives humans a place in the creation above all other creatures. We had even been given the biblical mandate to subjugate the earth to our designs. If we could not rid ourselves entirely of our instinctuality, our animalistic body functions, at least we could consider those things undignified, as belonging to a realm, bounded by shame and unworthy of discussion.

Something a young woman told me in the early 1950s provides a good illustration of this. She had a tendency to become involved in symbiotic love relationships and told me that she knew of an antidote to the violent and unwanted loves she often experienced. She had only to imagine the man of her dreams in long underwear or sitting on the toilet, wiping his posterior, to feel completely disgusted and disillusioned. (At the time, I suspect that such a graphic example would have been censored by any serious publisher – being beneath the dignity of an academically reputable publication. Today it would be considered undignified for a publisher or author to suppress such "naked" truths – so far have the boundaries of shame shifted in four decades).

Of course, many people are still too ashamed to let others know they underwent a hemorrhoidal, prostate, or gynecological procedure. I am reminded of a well-known elderly woman who died from coronary failure while sitting on the toilet. Some of her feces remained to be seen – and probably smelled as well. The family chose to censure this fact, reporting instead that her body had been discovered in the hallway. Otherwise, they reasoned, hers would have been an undignified death – making it difficult to hold a dignified memory of her. Such boundaries of shame are understandable. But the general effort to establish a less inhibited relationship to different parts of the body is a healthy development.

To investigate further the various elements that make up this feeling of personal dignity, we might ask ourselves what aspects of ourselves we are proud of. Then we could ask what aspects of behavior we would rather hide from ourselves and others. These are, to begin with, questions of self-representation: what conscious or unconscious self-image informs my conduct? Second, they are questions that bring to light the judgment that I assign to this image. Self-judgment usually takes place without conscious reflection; I spontaneously allow certain aspects of myself to come up for review while keeping other parts out of sight. Thus such judgments are usually made according to an unquestioned value system that exercises its influence unconsciously. Feelings of personal worth and dignity may be based on values that vary greatly from person to person and culture to culture. But one thing is common to every loss of dignity: the feeling of shame it promotes.

THE CONCEPT OF SELF: SENSE OF SELF, CONSCIOUSNESS OF SELF

As I have said, the multifaceted theme of the self has met with mounting interest in recent years and has been the subject of discussion in countless books and articles (e.g. Fordham 1986, Gordon 1985, Jacoby 1990, Kohut 1971a, 1977, Redfearn 1985). Here I would like to address a few points from this literature that are relevant to our topic.

We might begin with the idea of the self as it is understood in psychoanalysis. Here, self is interpreted to mean "myself," the way I experience myself as a whole person, both in my conscious and unconscious ideas about myself (Hartmann 1964: 127). Psychoanalysts speak of "self-representation," meaning the way my personality is represented in fantasy. My fantasies of myself conform well enough with reality to contribute flexibly to my self-realization and productively to self-evaluation. But the way I represent myself in fantasies may also

26

reflect a distorted, overblown, understated, shifting, or impoverished image of myself. Then there is the question of whether I can have a relatively objective view of my self that takes into account both my dark and rosy sides. Or is the act of evaluation itself distorting? In other words, do I have a more or less realistic assessment of myself and my personality, or is there a disturbance in my self-perception and self-assessment? Who judges and evaluates whom? Can we trust that judging "voice" in us to be more or less objective? And upon what criteria are its judgments based?

Such questions have to be asked over a course of psychotherapeutic treatment whenever the analysand makes self-deprecating remarks that sound destructive and that do not correspond to the image that I as an analyst have of him. When I ask who it is that makes such judgments, and according to what criteria, the analysand often realizes that he first heard such judgments from significant others early in life, and then unconsciously adopted them as his own. "Identification with the aggressor" is a common defense mechanism that is unconsciously employed in order to disarm potential enemies (as well as the analyst). Thus, one attempts to forestall an unfavorable judgment from the outside by doing it to oneself first within. Obviously, it is helpful to make such mechanisms conscious. This task describes what is literally meant by the term "analysis." It is a process of separating unconscious mixtures into their component elements, for example differentiating between one's own self-evaluation and judgments made by significant others in the past. Such analyses and their attendant insights can be of great value. But when we are dealing with disturbances of self-esteem, differentiated insights are quickly absorbed again in an all-encompassing feeling of worthlessness. The roots of this feeling usually go much deeper than any convincing insight. Differentiation between a realistic self-perception and all kinds of distorting judgments made by an internalized authority figure (the "superego") is quickly blurred; the negative or positive values given to the self-image have an effect on our entire emotional state and influence in turn the way we perceive ourselves.

Now, I would like to distinguish between the sense of self as such and the feeling of self-esteem. In other words, I would like to touch upon the sense of self and how it comes into being before coming back to the problem of how one applies internal judgments to that self.

Mahler et al. described the sense of self as the earliest perception of one's existence as a separate entity. It is not the feeling of who I am, which would involve a comparison with others, an assessment, but simply the feeling that I am (Mahler et al. 1975: 8). I should point out that I am using the phrase "sense of self" in a non-technical way, because it comes closest to expressing the experience I have in mind: namely, the sense that it is I myself who acts, reacts, feels, and thinks. Nevertheless, more will need to

27

be said later on the important distinctions between the theoretical constructs of "I," "ego," and "self."

Theoretically, at least, we can distinguish between the feeling that I am and the feeling of who or how I am, – the latter always including the values I attribute to myself. Ego-functions and conscious intentions are based on the feeling that I am, i.e. my sense of self, and thus it seems relevant to consider the origins of the sense of self in early childhood.

I am interested, above all, in the views of modern infant researchers who believe they have discovered a subjective sense of self that long predates the existence of any image or representation of the self, indeed that is observable soon after the child is born. Here I rely especially on the work of Daniel Stern (1985), which draws upon not only his own clinical experience and research but that of other Americans working in the field. On the basis of this research, Stern arrived at certain hypotheses concerning the origin of a sense of self. In its earliest stages, the sense of self has nothing to do with reflective consciousness or speech. In the following pages, I would like to describe and discuss those points made by Stern that seem to be of particular relevance for our topic.

STAGES IN THE ORGANIZATION OF THE SENSE OF SELF: DANIEL STERN

Stern proposed a model for the emergence of the sense of self through developmental stages taking place in the "interpersonal world" of the infants. From the very beginning, he reports, this sense of "self" includes an "other"; it is always a sense of "self with other." For the infant, the "other" is its most important caretaker – in most cases the mother. This model of development differs from popular psychoanalytic views, which are based largely on the findings of Margaret Mahler. According to Mahler *et al.* (1975), after a brief, initial phase of "autism," the infant passes through a stage of symbiotic fusion with the mother (between the second and seventh month), after which it begins gradually to differentiate itself as a separate person. In contrast, Stern and other researchers have observed that infants are already able to distinguish between themselves and other people at birth. This explains why newborns are able to distinguish the smell of their own mother's milk from that of a "stranger" (Stern 1985: 39f). Infants also clearly prefer human faces to other visual patterns. In addition, the experimenters found they were able to enter into a dialogue with their tiny subjects in which the infants made such observable responses as turning their heads, sucking, looking at the experimenter, and looking away. Such experiments led Stern to have a series of insights about the mental experience of infants that challenges existing psychoanalytic theories of development.

From birth until the second month, the infant lives in a world that Stern calls the domain of the "emergent self." In this preliminary stage, particular events and perceptions are experienced as whole entities, but the newborn perceives them as separate moments with no cumulative relation to each other. Observing such discrete, unrelated experiences, other psychoanalytical thinkers have concluded that infants live in an undifferentiated state. However, according to Stern, the subjective life of the infant may consist of many distinct and vivid experiences. For now, we have no way of knowing whether the infant experiences a connection between these various experiences. But soon, these single moments begin organizing themselves into successively larger, more comprehensive structures. The infant experiences what Stern called an "emergent self" when an inner creative process begins, that brings the infant into the first domain of organized self-experience.

Stern called this first domain the sense of a "core self." He and other researchers observed that by the second month, a sense of self has already developed that allows the infant to experience intention and motivation as its own. At this point, the infant's sense of its own body, its boundaries, and its sense of coherence have also come alive. At the same time, it has the experience of being together with an "other" – the caretaker. These are not experiences of symbiotic fusion but, according to Stern, simply a way of coming together with "self-regulating others." The infant experiences changes in its own state coming about via the "other," for example through nursing, bathing, and the changing of diapers. A sense of the self that is associated with the need for security – bonding, mutual gazing, snuggling, and being held – is dependent on the caretaker. In spite of the fact that the infant's sense of self changes along with the activity of the caretaker, the boundary between self and other remains intact. This can be better described as relatedness to a "self-regulating other" than as a merging, though it is important to keep in mind that, in this phase, the infant's experience consists primarily of body-feeling and exchanges of physical intimacy.

Between the seventh and fifteenth month a capacity develops for actual interpersonal relatedness. Infants discover that they can share subjective experiences with someone else. While in the previous phase the infant's subjective experience was still determined by the mother's regulation, now the focus shifts to the need for common experience. The infant discovers which aspects of its experience can be shared and which cannot. At one end of a hypothetical spectrum of infant experience in this stage of a "subjective" sense of self, would be the feeling of psychic connectedness, at the other would be a sense of profound isolation, even a "cosmic loneliness" (Köhler 1988: 61). According to Stern's model, it is only now that fusion with the significant other is possible, while in the psycho-analytic view, the period of symbiosis began to recede at seven to nine months. The decisive factor at this stage is "affect attunement:" i.e., to what extent are mother and child able to attune themselves to each other's affects? Such an attunement assures the continued development of the infant's subjective sense of self and the emergence of the domain of intersubjectivity. At best, the mother's sensitive, affirming attitude allows the child to feel: "I know that you know how I am doing" (Köhler 1988: 64). Thus, in this stage of development, the human need to express oneself, to be seen, heard, and understood becomes central for the first time.

The age of fifteen to eighteen months initiates a new stage in the organization of the child's sense of self and its relatedness to the other. This burst of growth, coinciding with the acquisition of language, could be likened to a revolution. It begins with the infant's capacity to take itself as the object of its own reflection. Thus, an "objective self" comes into being next to the "subjective self" of earlier phases. The propensity of children of this age to look with fascination at their own reflection in the mirror is a clear indication of this phase, as is the development of the capacity for symbolic play. Through language, issues such as bonding, autonomy, separation, and intimacy, are practiced with the significant other at a level not previously possible.

But language is a double-edged sword. On the one hand it enriches the field of common experience, on the other hand, limits it. Only part of the original global experience can be expressed in words; the rest remains inaccurately named and poorly understood. Many other realms of experience remain likewise unexpressed, left to lead a nameless but nonetheless very real existence. Language thus drives a wedge between two modes of experience: one that can only be lived directly, and another that can be verbally represented. To the extent that experience is connected to words, the growing child becomes shut off from the spontaneous flow of experience that had characterized the preverbal state. Thus the child gains entry into its culture at the cost of losing the strength and wholeness of its original experience. Stern describes this development as follows:

> The self becomes a mystery. The infant is aware that there are levels and layers of self-experience that are to some extent estranged from the official experiences ratified by language. The previous harmony is broken.

> (Stern 1985: 272)

This crisis in self-comprehension occurs because, for the first time in its life, the infant experiences the self as divided and rightly senses that no one can heal this split (Stern 1985: 272).

Stern thus described four organizational stages in the development of a sense of self: the emergent self, the core self, the subjective self, and the verbal self. But he emphasized, quite importantly in my view, that these points of crystallization are not strictly bounded. The various structures comprising the child's sense of self may develop in succession, each having its own period of formation and vulnerability. However, the higher stages do not simply replace the previous ones. Once a particular quality in the sense of self has been established, it remains for the rest of one's life. In other words, there are four fundamental ways of being in the world. Over a lifetime, these can develop, differentiate, become renewed or enriched, but they can also remain undifferentiated, atrophy, or split off to an extent.

Stern uses the experience of making love to illustrate these four coexisting domains.

> Making love, a fully involving interpersonal event, involves first the sense of the self and the other as discrete physical entities, as forms in motion – an experience in the domain of core-relatedness, as is the sense of self-agency, will, and activation encompassed in the physical acts. [I would like to add that each partner mutually influences and alters the state of the other's bodily self-experience. MJ]
>
> At the same time it involves the experience of sensing the other's subjective state: shared desire, aligned intentions, and mutual states of simultaneously shifting arousal, which occur in the domain of intersubjective relatedness. And if one of the lovers says for the first time "I love you," the words summarize what is occurring in the other domains (embraced in the verbal perspective) and perhaps introduce an entirely new note about the couple's relationship that may change the meaning of the history that had led up to and will follow the moment of saying it. This is an experience in the domain of verbal relatedness.

> (Stern 1985: 30)

I would add that lovers tend to create an idiomatic language of interaction that may bear a certain resemblance to the dialogue between mother and child. This sort of language facilitates an instinctive emotional exchange, while a highly abstract language, aimed only at the "head," would hinder such an exchange.

> What about the domain of emergent relatedness? That is less readily apparent, but is present nonetheless. One may, for example "get lost in" the color of the other's eye, as if the eyes were momentarily not part of the core other, unrelated to anyone's mental state, newly found, and outside of any larger organizing network. At the instant the "colored eye" comes again to belong to the known other, an emergent experience has occurred, an experience in the domain of emergent relatedness.

> (Stern 1985: 30–1)

THE GENESIS OF HUMAN PATTERNS OF INTERACTION

When the infant's experiences of a "self-regulating other" repeat themselves, they become recorded in memory and internalized, in a more general form, as ideas and expectations. In other words, they become internal psychic representations, which Stern (in his American style) calls by the acronym RIGs: "representations of interactions that have been generalized." These RIGs are not isolated images of mother and father, nor representations of "self" and "object"; but rather they are fantasies and expectations about interactions with significant others. For the child, they form an inner knowledge garnered from experience about how the activities of the other (caretaker) affect its state – whether through stimulation, satisfaction, fright or pain. Since these ideas or representations are active with or without verbalization, the child can evoke its companion even when alone. For example, a child may have had fun playing with its mother. Later, it expresses pleasure playing on its own, due to the "historical result of similar past moments in the presence of a delight- and exuberance-enhancing (regulating) other" (Stern 1985: 113). The reaction that originally took place only in the presence of the other now repeats itself independently of her. As Stern writes:

> The infant's life is so thoroughly social that most of the things the infant does, feels, and perceives occur in different kinds of relationships. An evoked companion ... or fantasied union with mother is no more or less than the history of specific kinds of relationships or the prototypic memory of many specific ways of being with mother.
>
> (Stern 1985: 118)

Of course the mother also has her own ideas and expectations of interaction. Her "evoked companion" includes not only the child, but also, in an experiential background derived from earlier interactions, her own mother. Mother's own maternal fantasies enter into the interaction with her child as well. There are also areas in which the subjective worlds of mother and infant overlap.

According to Stern, the subjective experience of the child is largely social, regardless of whether the child is actually with others or alone. From an introverted perspective, however, this statement can only be valid if one defines "self-regulating other" broadly enough to include intrapsychic images and ideas, as does Kohut to some extent in his concept of the "self object." To my mind, it is important to emphasize that the inner representations take on a more or less generalized form and are not limited to association with the personal mother. From a Jungian standpoint, we could attribute our capacity to form a general "representation" or inner image out of countless independent experiences to a creative, structuring power called the archetype.

This concludes my brief summary of hypotheses by infant researchers, so vividly described by Stern, that seem relevant to my theme. I hope the reader has found Stern's points as persuasive as I have. The work gives us new insights not only into mother and infant interactions, but all kinds of relational structures in which individuals become involved – including the analytical situation. That is how I justify the relatively detailed synopsis given here. Readers familiar with models of early childhood development worked out by psychoanalytic or Jungian writers (e.g. Neumann 1988, Fordham 1969, 1976) will ask themselves, as I do, how these models relate to Stern's, which is "correct," and whether they are not mutually contradictory.

This question has concerned me a great deal. Indeed, it has dawned on me that in this area I am very much in what Stern describes as the domain of an "emergent self." This is a realm characterized by a sense of disconnection between separate parts of experience, which are like islands that would like to grow together into a continent. In the realm of the "emerging self," in other words, a central core has not yet become solid enough to allow for integration of the separate parts. Of course, the need to integrate various parts into a whole is archetypal, representing one of humanity's most fundamental concerns: the quest for a unity underlying diversity (Samuels 1989: 33ff; Spiegelman 1989: 53ff). However, my objective here is not to write a theoretical treatise comparing various concepts of the self, but to explore self-esteem and its relation to shame-anxiety. For those interested in a comparative discussion and hypothetical integration of various concepts of the self, I have provided some thoughts in an appendix. I would also refer interested readers to a relevant chapter in my book *Individuation and Narcissism* (Jacoby 1990).

THE PSYCHOGENESIS OF SELF-ESTEEM

As said before, self-esteem is the basic value I attribute to my personality. This assessment is deeply rooted in the unconscious, and is only alterable within limits. With high self-esteem, I have a good, satisfied, "loving" feeling about my self-image – the fantasy I have of myself. Self-deprecation and feelings of inferiority stem from a correspondingly negative evaluation. Again, such self judgments are closely bound up with the evaluations and judgments significant others have made of us beginning early in life.

The patterns of fantasy described by Stern – fantasies etched by interactions between the self and the "self-regulating other" (RIGs) – are tremendously important in the psychogenesis of self-esteem – that is, in its emotional birth and the development of its various manifestations. Notwithstanding its own initiative and distinctness, the self of the infant is continually dependent on the "self-regulating other," and thus this "other" has an extremely decisive influence on the infant's state of being.

The formation of a healthy sense of self-esteem therefore depends on a good enough "match" and "mutual attunement" between infant and caretaker. Under the best of circumstances, small hints suffice to alert the caretaker to the infant's immediate needs – whether for changing, feeding or whatever. It is also essential that he be sensitive to moments when the infant wants to be left alone, for it already requires a certain amount of "private space in time" (Sander 1983) to pursue its own interests without guidance. In other words, an infant needs the opportunity to choose among a variety of possibilities for setting its activities into motion, developing initiative, and watching what happens. Donald Winnicott expressed the opinion that the capacity to be alone is based on a paradox – namely the experience of being alone in the presence of someone else.

> It is only when alone (that is to say, in the presence of someone) that the infant can discover his own personal life. The pathological alternative is a false life built up on reactions to external stimuli.
>
> (Winnicott 1958: 34)

It seems that by being sensitive to the infant's "private space," a caretaker helps the child establish healthy patterns of interaction. If the child could talk, it might express its corresponding feelings this way: "I have the permission and the right to have free time and space to pursue my own activities. This does not necessarily disturb others; in fact, they welcome it. I can be myself, can be true to myself, even when I am with others." Or: "I don't insult anyone even if I am not always communicative and plugged in to them. If I have nothing to say, no one is going to feel awkward or hurt."

Caretakers are not always able to provide the infant with this free space because they themselves need the infant's affirmation of love too much. Or their anxiety does not allow them to relax their constant, controlling care. Experiences with such needy or anxious caretakers give rise to patterns of interaction that, if the infant could speak, might be rendered thus: "I am only accepted under the condition that I constantly show my love and care for others. Spontaneity is dangerous; everything must be kept rigidly under control." This pattern of interaction is evident in persons who suffer from dependency, passivity, and lack of initiative. In Jungian terminology, this condition is called a "dominance of the mother complex." Some caretakers resent having to be always there for the "crybaby" and the restriction this puts on their freedom to pursue their own personal interests. Such an attitude may well impair the quality of care a person is able to bring to a child, who probably will go away feeling that: "I must be thankful that anyone spends any time with me at all. Sooner or later I will be left alone. Basically I am a bother and a nuisance to others."

Of course, many different kinds of relationships can develop between caretaker and child, but a relatively frequent pattern is one in which the quality of relatedness shifts according to the caretaker's mood. Periods of harmonious mutuality are suddenly disrupted by the withdrawal of parental attention and caring. As a result, the infant's interactional patterns may be marked by a basic mistrust, a sense of the unreliability of others and oneself. Of course, fluctuations are unavoidable in the climate between two persons; indeed they are part of a process of "optimal frustration" necessary for maturation. But an infant that cannot depend on a certain continuity of attention and empathic care, in spite of its own constant efforts, loses its basic trust and self-confidence. In other words, when the "self-regulating other" is unreliable, the infant experiences too much fluctuation in its sense of self-esteem.

An infant's wishes to understand and to be understood first manifest themselves during the development of the subjective sense of self and its domain of intersubjectivity. At that time, a need arises in the child for mutual expression of subjective experience such that every thwarting of that need can have a very negative effect. Parents are already socializing the infant in a particular way when, consciously or unconsciously, they respond empathically to certain not-yet verbal expressions and either fail to notice or dismiss others with certain disdainful gestures. As mentioned, this is the stage when the infant is first exploring which aspects of its private world may be communicated and which are better withheld. Depending on the results of these explorations, there will either be a sense of psychic commonality or a sense that the world holds little or no understanding, and an accompanying sense of isolation. Thus the question of which parts of the inner universe can be shared is a matter of the greatest importance. Some experiences cannot be shared because they are subject to a taboo, an unspoken "Don't touch that." Here are the preverbal origins of such judgmental "inner voices" as, "We don't talk about such things," or even, "We don't think about such things."

One might object that much of the foregoing may be a projection of adult fantasies onto infants. Could the infant really be so sensitive to the judgments of others? An experiment devised by Emde would indicate that it is – i.e., that infants in this phase sense the reactions of their caretakers and attune themselves accordingly (see Stern 1985: 132). In the experiment, an infant is brought to a "visual cliff," an optical illusion that causes a certain amount of fear. Typically the infant hesitates, unsure whether or not to continue crawling, then it looks to its parent and adopts his affective facial expression as its guideline. If the parent smiles, the infant crawls on with a happy expression. If he shows fear, the infant stays where it is. Thus, one may conclude that at nine months, many infants have already developed a refined sense of which of its modes of expression and activity are desirable and which are not.

I believe that neurotic shame-reactions may first make their appearance at this phase – whenever the infant's communications or activities meet with serious disapproval. Parental disgust at anal excretions is only one kind of rejection. If an infant disturbs its parent by touching its stool, crying at the wrong moment, showing fear, or shrieking with joy, he may not have to say anything for the infant to hear the message: "Shame on you," and "If you keep on like that, you are certainly not the good little child we wanted and expected." When there is too much emphasis on the caretaker's subjective reactions and too little empathy for the infant's emotional state, affect attunement remains fragmentary at best. This situation may prompt in the infant the following pattern of interaction: "I really have to accommodate myself to everyone else if I don't want to be in the wrong place at the wrong time – if I don't want to feel ashamed of myself and unwanted. I would do better to avoid this danger completely by holding back all spontaneous expressions." More severe disturbances in the emotional encounter between caretaker and child would result in a "tape" such as, "No matter who I am, no matter what I say, I alienate everyone. No one will ever accept me, and if I seek relationship with others, I will meet with humiliating rejection."

When there is mutual agreement in the domain of intersubjective relatedness, the infant will also develop a sense of having an effect on the experience of the other. But children that have been damaged in this domain often cannot believe that they can be important to others simply by virtue of their existence and the radiance of their natural being. They imagine that they must make gifts and do good deeds in order to earn the love of others; at the very least, they feel that they must accomplish outstanding achievement in order to be accepted. They may long for someone to love them for their own sake, but believe this remote desire has little justification or hope of fulfillment.

Disturbances at the stage of preverbal intersubjectivity may also have the apparently opposite effect: in a compensatory fashion, persons who are wounded in this domain may force themselves on others to make sure they get the attention that is their due. They will do anything, from demonstrative sulking to brash displays of power.

In any case it is in the domain of intersubjectivity that emotional abandonment might take place, leaving the child with a serious deficit in the area of self-esteem (see also Asper 1993).

When significant others take pride in the small child's growing capacity for verbal expression, a pattern of interaction is established that promotes growth and stimulates a joy in linguistic expression. But some ambitious parents constantly correct their children, hoping to speed up their mastery of the language. This can create a pattern of interaction expressed by the following "tape": "Every time I say something the way it spontaneously comes out, I am criticized. I always have to watch what I say." Depending on one's innate rhetorical talents, this programming may lead to elegant discourse in adulthood. But just as often, it can be experienced as an impossible expectation, inhibiting spontaneous verbal expression and creating a sense of inferiority.

Many parents are justifiably glad when their child gradually "becomes reasonable" in the domain of the verbal sense of self. But a child-rearing philosophy that overemphasizes reasonable explanations can be danger-ous. When this lopsided emphasis on reason overshadows the more emotional approach of mutual attunement, large portions of the child's psyche are not heard, and the child feels abandoned. Overly intellectual parents, or parents who suffer from narcissistic disturbances of empathy, are at a loss in the domain of intersubjectivity. They are thus under-standably relieved when their child finally submits to "reason." This situation may give rise to the following pattern of interaction: "My need for soul-connection, for a feeling- or intuition-based approach to myself and the world, falls upon deaf ears. Thus, this whole domain must be of no value; what counts is reason and reasonable negotiation in all matters. To take feelings seriously and try to share them only brings embarrassment." Consciously or unconsciously, the child comes to expect that he will not be understood, and to fear rejection and devaluation.

I realize that my discussion of the origins and development of self-esteem has focused largely on potential problem areas. I attribute this to the *déformation professionelle* of the psychotherapist, who mostly encounters disturbances. But a study of deficiency symptoms can shed light on the conditions necessary for the development of a realistic sense of self-worth. To summarize: the development of healthy self-esteem depends on the caretaker's love for the infant's very existence, both its psychic and physical expressions. But that is not all. As Stern emphasizes, mutual attunement depends on more than the good will of the caretaker. Some-times temperamental differences make it nearly impossible for "affect attunement" to take place between parent and child. Moreover, infants are differently endowed with vitality and with the ability to reach out and get the care and attention they need. Then again, not every child can express its native essence and joy in a way that the caretaker can welcome. Thus, I believe that parents should not become unduly insecure by reading psychological literature. Often the very fear of "not doing it right" will cause a stiffening of their emotional and intuitive interactions with their child. The ideal of the "perfect parent" is often counterproductive, as Christa Rohde-Dachser suggested in her essay, "Farewell to the Guilt of the Mothers" (1989).

Given this caveat, the basic ideas described here concerning the influence of early interactions between child and caretaker on the development of self-esteem are certainly important. Still, the life of the psyche is too complex to be satisfactorily explained by a few basic patterns. Such factors as defenses and compensations also need to be considered.

An interesting, but more theoretical psychological question would be: to what degree do patterns of interaction established in the various domains of the sense of self have an archetypal quality? To what extent are these patterns at the basis not only of interpersonal but of intrapsychic communication – that is, communication between the ego and the "figures" of the unconscious? Though I cannot pursue this question here, I would like to remind the reader of Erich Neumann's description of "archetypal stages of development." Neumann said the Self (using that word in the Jungian sense) was the center of the personality, guiding the child through the various archetypal stages of development. But he rightly added:

> The evocation of the archetypes and the related release of latent psychic developments are not only intrapsychic processes; they take place in an archetypal field which embraces inside and outside and which always includes and presupposes an outside stimulus – a world factor.
>
> (Neumann 1988: 82)

According to Neumann, the first "world factor" was in the mother and the "primal relationship." The success of that relationship would determine whether or not an "integral ego" could develop.

> There arises a positive tolerance on the part of the ego which, on the basis of its attitude of security and confidence toward the mother, is capable of accepting the world and itself, because it has a constant experience of positive tolerance and acceptedness through the mother.
>
> (Neumann 1988: 58–9)

In other words, a pattern of interaction is established that is infused with the basic fantasy, "I am loved, cared for, and valued by others the way I am." A foundation is laid for the development of healthy self-confidence and the construction of a "positive ego-Self axis" (Neumann 1988).

From the viewpoint of depth psychology as a general rule, a realistic enough sense of self-respect depends on good enough parenting. Infant research mainly emphasizes the interpersonal world and brings to our attention the infant's own active influence on the relationship with the parent. Those periods in which the various forms of self-experience first manifest themselves naturally have a determining influence on the infant's subsequent experience of self and world. But new developments are constantly occurring in every domain of the self that extends over the course of the entire lifespan. Thus, therapy must not confine itself to a search for the origins of disturbances in the earliest formative periods. New experiences are always possible, indeed inevitable, in the ongoing stream of life, and these may modify the original internal patterns. If this were not so, psychotherapy would hardly be effective (Stern 1985: 273ff).

MIRRORING AND THE FORMATION OF IDEALS

Thus far, we have paid little attention to a phenomenon that greatly influences self-esteem, namely the so-called "ego ideal" or "ideal self." Stern has not written about the process of idealization, because this process may not begin until after the onset of the verbal phase and would therefore lie outside the scope of his research. However, the "self psychology" of Heinz Kohut does recognize the important process of idealization (Kohut 1971a, 1977). According to Kohut, a cohesive self comes into being, in part, when the infant's spontaneous "exhibitionistic" activities meet with its parent's joyful and empathic mirroring. The phrase Kohut uses again and again to describe this phenomenon is "the gleam in mother's eye." In other words, optimal parental empathy lays the foundation for a healthy feeling of self-worth, one that allows a child to win and hold on to a "place in the sun" without compulsive ambition, but also without inhibition, shame, or guilty feelings about being "seen" or exposed in an embarrassing way. In my opinion, one's need "to be respected and highly regarded," to enjoy a certain "distinction" in the world, is bound up with one's earliest relation to the "gleam in mother's eye."

Stern, Neumann, and Kohut – along with D.W. Winnicott, Michael Fordham, and others – all agree that a successful early mother–child relationship is vital to the construction of a healthy feeling of self-worth. For the practitioner, it makes little difference whether the maternal caretaker, carrying out the work of "self-regulating other" (Stern) is called "incarnated functional realm of the Self" (Neumann) or "selfobject" (Kohut). Because such terms reveal the different emphases of various theoretical schools, they are of a certain interest for developmental psychology, but they are not so crucial for the practice of therapy. What the practitioner must possess is a well-rounded knowledge of insights from developmental psychology that will enable him to empathically understand the patient's childhood wounds.

According to Kohut, something else occurs as the self is forming. Not only does the self desire to be admired and empathically understood by the "selfobject" (its caretaker); it experiences this selfobject (father or mother) as omnipotent and perfect. Since, in Kohut's view, the selfobject can hardly be distinguished from the self's own world, the perfection attributed to the selfobject implies the child's own perfection. The infant in a sense fuses with the selfobject, which it experiences as idealized, omnipotent, and perfect. Disappointment over the gradual realization that one's parents were hardly all-knowing, all-powerful, and perfect, can effect a "transmuting internalization," which creates structures that can become a matrix for developing ideals. (In Jungian terms, this would be called the withdrawal of projections.)

In other words, self-esteem can be created and maintained by means of the ideals that emerge out of a fusion with an idealized "selfobject." These ideals are convincing and can become models for one's own conduct. One thinks here of people who work very hard at worthy and meaningful tasks – large or small – losing themselves completely in a higher cause. Such people often cannot admit that their noble service increases their sense of self-worth considerably. Consciously, they are only aware of a "selfless devotion" to broadly human, scientific, creative, religious, or social ideas that give their lives meaning.

This brings to mind the famous syndrome of the "helper," whose theme could be expressed as follows: "Let me be there for you with all my power, for that is my task in life." The fact that the helper's own self-esteem stands or falls with his ability to do the task is overlooked, since such an admission would amount to confession of an "egoistic shadow" masquerading in such ideals. This shadow prefers that its power remain hidden in a closet of shame. In a process of self-discovery, such a person must sooner or later confront the reality that the ideal of pure altruism always breaks down under the limits of being human.

Of course, these observations should not be taken as criticisms, meant to discourage us from undertaking tasks transcending our personal needs. Today more than ever, such devotion is urgently needed. If performing it contributes to one's feelings of self-worth, so much the better. After all, the boundaries between the ego ideal and the so-called "grandiose self" are very flexible.

An illustration would be the sense of importance I get from doing altruistic or self-sacrificial work for the sake of some global issue or the welfare of others – without noticing (or by being forced to notice in an embarrassing way) how great I seem to myself while doing it. These sorts of realizations suggest that we need to direct our attention to the phenomenology and effects of the grandiose self.

SELF-ESTEEM AND THE GRANDIOSE SELF

The so-called "grandiose self," whose effects are largely unconscious, is a factor underlying a variety of disturbances of self-esteem. Thus it is the two most important researchers in the field of narcissism – Otto F. Kernberg (1975) and Heinz Kohut (1971a) – whose names are most closely associated with the concept of the grandiose self, though the two have offered differing interpretations of its psychodynamics.

Kohut believes the grandiose self represents a fixation at the stage of an archaic yet normal childhood self characterized by unlimited – albeit illusory – omnipotence and omniscience. It is an intrapsychic "structure" formed in early childhood around which fantasies of omniscience, omnipotence, and unlimited perfection are entwined. Under favorable conditions, the child learns in subsequent stages of maturity to recognize and accept its limits. Then, grandiose fantasies are replaced, one by one, with a more or less realistic feeling of self-worth.

As I have said, such favorable development depends largely on the child's receiving empathic mirroring from significant others. If, however, this process is disturbed – and with it, the integration of the grandiose self – this psychic structure can be split off from the ego and its reality testing, or separated from these by means of repression (Kohut 1971a: 108). Then the grandiose self is no longer open to modification, but remains in its archaic form, all the while exerting its influence from the unconscious. "A persistently active grandiose self with its delusional claims may severely incapacitate an ego of average endowment," wrote Kohut, although he added that a minimally modified grandiose self can spur highly gifted persons on to their most outstanding achievements (Kohut 1971a: 108–9). The grandiose self, in Kohut's view, is not of pathological proportions in every case.

For Kernberg, on the other hand, the grandiose self is a

> pathological condensation of some aspects of the real self (the "specialness" of the child reinforced by early experience), the ideal self (the fantasies and self images of power, wealth, omniscience, and beauty which compensated the small child for the experience of severe oral frustration, rage and envy) and the ideal object (the fantasy of an ever-giving, ever-loving and accepting parent, in contrast to the child's experience in reality; a replacement of the devalued real parental object).
>
> (Kernberg 1975: 265–6)

It is clear that Kernberg's observations and hypotheses concerning the grandiose self do not necessarily describe the same mental phenomena as do Kohut's. In Kernberg's view, the grandiose self originates in a defense in which the ego, identifying with this sense of grandiosity, staves off all close human relationships and causes isolating loneliness. This form of grandiose self is part of a phenomenon that Kernberg calls "pathological narcissism." The self-worth of one afflicted with this condition rests in the illusion of one's particular greatness. Lacking trust, such a person keeps others at a distance or devalues them as long as they do not play the part of an admiring echo. In spite of his grandiose fantasies, however, the pathological narcissist retains the capacity for reality-testing.

The whole problem of the grandiose self in relation to disturbances of self-esteem requires further elaboration. It seems to me that most people have secret fantasies of grandiosity, whose effects unravel themselves from the unconscious. But these fantasies are often guarded with feelings of shame, and are hardly ever admitted into consciousness, let alone verbalized. One is ashamed to be seen as pretentious, and as a defense, one attempts to appear as humble as possible.

41

What is the difference between the "grandiose self" and the self in the Jungian sense? A few remarks are in order here. Ego development involves coming to grips with the limitations of one's personality, or realizing, as Margaret Mahler has pointed out, that "I am not perfect or omnipotent; I am small and 'dependent'." But this does not mean that "perfection" or "omnipotence" lose their influence as central archetypal fantasies. Rather, these qualities are projected onto and joined with one's image of God. Since only God is perfect and omnipotent, the personal ego can and must differentiate itself from the grandiose self, which appropriates those qualities to itself. The ego must be humble and shy in the face of the divinity – a requirement of practically every religion. "Hubris" – the desire to be divine – is regarded by most religions as the worst of all errors and an insult to God. When Jung equated the self with the image of God in the human soul, he took great pains to differentiate the ego from the Self. This must be repeatedly emphasized. For the sake of mental health, the ego should neither become identified with the Self nor "divinized," lest it succumb to "inflation.'

In early childhood, ego and Self (in the Jungian sense) are fairly closely fused. The ego has not yet become differentiated from the Self, or become a relatively autonomous center of consciousness. But when we speak of adults having a "grandiose self," we imply that there is a sector of their personality, too, in which the boundaries between ego and Self are not clearly marked. The conscious ego has a tendency either to become caught up in or to feel threatened by notions of perfection. Then, one's estimation of oneself becomes to some extent distorted. As I have said, there are probably few persons for whom, in some area of the personality, ego and Self do not occasionally fuse, leading to slight or serious fluctuations of self-esteem (see also Jacoby 1990: 93).

The intense effect of the grandiose Self on one's subjective state is a personal experience that precedes whatever psychodynamic perspective we apply to it. Persons who suffer from so-called "narcissistic grandiosity" identify to a certain extent with their grandiose selves, although their capacity for reality-testing and their fundamental sense of self (Stern) remain intact. (Complete identification with the grandiose self would result in psychotic delusions of grandeur.) But for many people, the fantasies of the grandiose self are embarrassing as well as enjoyable. These people feel their grandiose fantasies put them in the uncomfortable position of longing for esteem and admiration, while also fearing these things. They may have difficulty dealing with praise and compliments, since their desire to be admired is fraught with shame. And yet if they do not get the attention and admiration they want, they feel hurt and injured.

I would like to divide the effects of the grandiose self on self-esteem into three broad categories: 1) identification of the ego with the grandiose self;

2) the grandiose self as a stimulus to ambition and need for admiration; and 3) the grandiose self as impossible demand.

IDENTIFICATION OF THE EGO WITH THE GRANDIOSE SELF

Here one has a sense of being a very "special" person – unusually gifted, attractive, intelligent, or whatever value occupies the highest rung in our particular ladder. The fantasy of being admired by everyone in the world is an important part of this. Sometimes there is a belief that certain rules and limitations, while necessary for others in order that humans may live together, need not apply to oneself. Such a person considers himself an exception, and expects to be treated accordingly by others. In Jungian terms, this state would be called psychic inflation, meaning that the ego is "puffed up" (*aufgeblasen*) by an archetypal image.

Whatever it is called, such grandiosity causes a high-flying feeling that in extreme cases can lead to submanic behavior. When it results in a loss of reality-testing, we speak of delusions of grandeur or of manic psychosis. In the majority of cases, however, such grandiosity manifests itself mainly in airs and graces of every variety – examples of which abound not only in the world of film and theater, but also in sports, politics, and science. Many people at the height of their fame and glory find it difficult to muster the mental stamina to endure the constant adulation of a public that views them as luminous stars in the sky. One thinks of the tragedies of Marilyn Monroe, Maria Callas, or even gurus like Baghwan Rajneesh. A person whose ego is identified with the grandiose self requires continual confirmation from the outside; without real or, in emergencies, fantasized admirers, he loses his balance. When the identification of the ego with the gleam of the grandiose self is broken, all that remains is a feeling of emptiness. The slightest criticism or questioning can make a grandiose fantasy collapse like a house of cards.

Naturally it is necessary to evaluate what basis one's sense of one's own greatness may have in reality and the extent to which it may diverge from reality. After all, certain people are exceptional. We also witness temporary inflations, which provide a person with enough energy to accomplish certain achievements and later are modified by real self-esteem. Often, however, identification with the grandiose self is a compensation for the fear that one is actually a despised nothing deserving of endless shame.

THE GRANDIOSE SELF AS STIMULUS FOR AMBITION AND THE NEED TO BE ADMIRED

In this case, the ego is aware that it is far from having achieved what it might have. The grandiose self exerts intense pressure to follow its demands for perfection. As Kohut correctly observed, such demands can spur a naturally gifted person on to great heights of achievement, but usually they simply have the effect of overtaxing him. Under the pressure of the grandiose self, the ego may be unable to accept that "no master has ever yet fallen like a star out of heaven." Instead, it insists that one should be able to do everything right away – and much better than anyone else – otherwise feelings of shame and inferiority take over. This can happen in the widest variety of professional or creative contexts, often making it difficult for a person to patiently endure the stages that his life and education pass through.

The grandiose self is behind the impulse to strive for perfection and is thus an energizing force. If one is able to set realistic goals, this can be a genuine aid to achievement. But as soon as one becomes driven, needing to attain "greatness" at any price, it becomes destructive. In pathological cases, it can drive the person to fraud, chicanery and deceit.

THE GRANDIOSE SELF AS IMPOSSIBLE DEMAND

In this case, the grandiose self's demand for perfection results in a devastating critique of one's own shortcomings. In a previous book, I undertook a detailed examination of this aspect of the grandiose self, seeing it as one of the most serious effects of narcissistic disturbance (Jacoby 1990). Here, the personality is dominated by a largely unconscious notion of perfection, in light of which all that one is or does seems completely worthless. Only a very few individuals affected by this problem are aware that the roots of their merciless self-deprecation lie in their own grandiose fantasies. Most feel only pain and a sense of inferiority. If they do entertain fantasies of greatness, these individuals are not likely to admit, and less likely to verbalize them. Because such fantasies are so heavily laden with shame, interpreting them in analysis requires great tact and sensitivity on the part of the therapist. Without such tact, the patient is likely to see such comments as disparaging accusations and to feel not only inferior and inadequate because of them, but guilty of ridiculous fantasies of grandiosity. The limitless demands of the grandiose self inhibit all creative endeavors, because they subject every attempt at expression to merciless criticism. Feelings of inferiority and shame do not promote expression of one's own ideas.

In the psyches of such persons, an early childhood pattern of interaction may still be in effect in which a parental figure or figures placed inordinately high demands on their child, resulting in mutual disappointment. The child's feelings of "omnipotence" met too early with a "knowing better" attitude on the part of his unempathic parents, resulting in the basic feeling that: "I cannot really live up to the demands of life, and it is hopeless to try to change the situation."

In such persons, the grandiose self ridicules every ounce of ambition and paralyzes every spark of initiative, fearing that these might be judged disparagingly. In more serious cases, the individual may be plagued by depression and an underlying feeling that he has no right to exist. Erich Neumann, who saw this attitude as the result of a damaged "primal relationship" (*Urbeziehung*), offered the following description:

> The Great Mother Figure of the primal relationship is a goddess of fate who, by her favor or disfavor, decided over life and death, positive or negative development; and moreover, her attitude is the supreme judgment, so that her defection is identical with a nameless guilt on the part of the child.
>
> (Neumann 1988: 87)

In my experience, the psychological effect of such an omnipotent, deprecating authority is more than a feeling of nameless guilt. It also means being ashamed at every turn. If one has no right to exist, it would be better not to be seen. One feels one is somehow leprous, needing to be ashamed of even wanting to belong to the human race, let alone making any claims on life or other persons. Of course, claims cannot be repressed completely, and so they come out in indirect, complex, and ambivalent ways, such that one's partner can hardly fulfill them.

Here I have described the phenomenon of narcissistic depression, which can be seen as an extreme case of damaged self-esteem wherein one's sense of self-worth is preyed upon by a merciless, rejecting, and repudiating grandiose self.

The grandiose self will require further discussion – especially as regards the question of how to deal psychotherapeutically with its various effects and manifestations. However, this concludes my remarks on the origins of self-esteem and its disturbance.

4

THE PSYCHOGENESIS OF
SHAME AND SUSCEPTIBILITY
TO SHAME

In this chapter, I will focus on various aspects of shame and susceptibility to shame, including its neurotic aspects. I would like to begin by summarizing the most important viewpoints that have been proposed on the subject. Shame exercises an essential function; without shame and the restraint it imposes, even the most rudimentary form of civilization would be unthinkable. Shame is a highly complex phenomenon, promoting the individual's adaptation to collective norms and morals no less than the protection of his privacy. In this respect, shame can be likened to a border guard who punishes those who overstep a particular moral code's sense of dignity and respectability. Transgression of such borders offends good morals and can result in social sanctions or at the very least, a certain loss of face.

Shame also sets boundaries on interpersonal contact, thus protecting individuality and identity. Shame can be an accurate gauge of the emotions that regulate closeness and distance in our most intimate relationships.

Thus shame has two very different functions. Following Aristotle's distinction, we must differentiate between those things that produce shame because they offend general opinion and those that are shameful because they harm the plain truth. In the first case, we have violated a mandate to behave according to social norms and expectations; in the second, we have violated an inner, psychic system of values. Thus shame in one aspect aids social adaptation, while in another aspect it preserves personal integrity. The potential for conflict between these two aspects is fundamental to the nature of human beings and leads to confrontations basic to the process of individuation.

Such confrontations are often a matter of questioning a moral code that one has adopted without reflection. One may need to de-absolutize a collective, internalized standard of values in order to alter the threshold of shame. In such a process of emancipation, things that were once shameful may come to elicit new responses. At best, a shift may take place in favor of personal integrity and the plain truth, preparing the way for a confrontation with general opinion.

SHAME AS INNATE AFFECT

Shame, it has been said, is an emotion inherent in human beings – an archetypal experience. Nevertheless, each individual has a unique developmental history of shame. Thus, an important question concerns how far back we can trace the roots of shame in the life of the child. Here the research of Tomkins (1963), who observed the first signs of shame in 6–8-month-old infants, is of interest. Spitz (1965) also noticed what he described as a fear of strange faces, the so-called "eight-month anxiety," in infants of this age.

> If a stranger approaches him, this will release an unmistakable, characteristic and typical behavior in the child; he shows varying intensities of apprehension or anxiety and rejects the stranger. Still, the individual child's hehavior varies over a rather wide range. He may lower his eyes "shyly," he may cover them with his hands, lift his dress to cover his face, throw himself prone on his cot and hide his face in the blankets, he may weep or scream. The common denominator is a refusal of contact, a turning away, with a shading, more or less pronounced, of anxiety.
>
> (Spitz 1965: 150)

Tomkins (1963), as well as Nathanson (1987a) viewed signs of contact-refusal (what Spitz calls "anxiety") as typical features of the basic emotion of shame/shyness. On the basis of these features, Tomkins described shame as an innate affect (Nathanson 1987a: 12), to be distinguished from fear, another innate affect (see also Izard 1977). This would suggest that next to, or even in place of, anxiety the first signs of shame appear at the age of 6–8 months, if not earlier.

According to Spitz, eight-month anxiety is an indication that the infant has gained the capacity to differentiate between its mother's face and those of strangers, a capacity which some researchers now place even earlier. In any case, this anxiety or shame-response seems quite understandable considering that eye contact and "face-to-face" relatedness are of decisive importance for any sort of bonding. Infants normally take great interest and joy in exploring their mothers' faces. If a child turns to its mother in the expectation of meeting the "gleam in her eye" (Kohut), but meets instead with a strange face, its curious, expectant engagement is abruptly broken. The infant's reaction has all the characteristics of shame that we know from the experience of adults.

On the basis of these observations, Tomkins hypothesized that the first signs of shame (as innate affect) always appear in connection with activated interest. Interest and joy are among those innate affects endowed with a positive feeling-tone, as opposed to negatively-toned innate affects, such as shame. Since, according to Tomkins's hypothesis, shame always follows upon interest in something, it has the function of setting boundaries to interest and the need to explore – which otherwise could become excessive.

I must admit that at first I had some difficulty with this hypothesis, which attributes the infant's earliest shame reactions to nothing more serious than its mistaking a strange face for that of its mother. I realized that as adults we have all felt the embarrassment of waving to an approaching person who we think is a friend only to discover that it is someone quite different. But still I wonder, could this embarrassment really originate in such an early mechanism of innate shame? The hypothesis that shame's function is to set boundaries on the infant's "interest," with its accompanying exploratory behavior and/or extravagant joy, became more plausible to me when I recognized similarities between this affect and Winnicott's description of early childhood "concern." The latter, Winnicott says, manifests itself initially at the same age and forms the basis for the future development of consideration for other persons (Winnicott 1963).

In his research, Spitz found that different infants express eight-month anxiety in different ways and with various degrees of intensity. Thus he posed the question, "May we assume that the differences in individual behavior are somehow connected with the affective climate in which the child was raised?" (Spitz 1965: 150). Tomkins also viewed as self-evident the proposition that innate shame develops from an innate stimulus–response mechanism into a learned and more generalized form of behavior. From the moment a child learns to distinguish its mother's face from that of a stranger, according to Tomkins, "shame is inevitable for any human being insofar as desire outruns fulfillment sufficiently to attenuate interest without destroying it" (Tomkins 1963: 185).

To round out Spitz's observations and Tomkins's hypothesis, I think we should also grant the possibility that the infant's anxiety or shame can be caused not only by the face of a stranger, but also by the "strange" face of its own parent or caretaker.[2] Even the good enough parent is subject to moods, making it unlikely he will always turn to his child with the same, familiar face. This would help us understand the frequent connection between unreliable paternal mirroring and susceptibility to shame. When a parent does not share his infant's joyfully communicated interest, his face will seem somewhat strange (or alienating as adults might say). The resulting feeling of rejection, interruption of contact, or of being thrust back onto oneself can have the effect of shaming the infant and need not be expressed in words in order to have an impact.

In my opinion, these considerations add credibility to Tomkins's supposition of a relationship between "stranger-anxiety" and the mechanisms that produce early shame. Who has not felt disappointed when a matter of greatest importance to us fails to interest someone we are close to, leaving us high and dry, raising doubts as to whether the matter has any value at all? In my practice, I find that analysands often refrain from raising emotionally important issues because they are afraid – consciously or unconsciously – that they might alienate me, and thus bring disgrace and ridicule upon themselves. On the other hand, it is an essential function of social behavior to set limits on shameless curiosity and the instinct to explore – even on boundless joy, if it somehow impinges upon others. Few persons wish to be seen as intrusive, curious, inconsiderate or imposing. Most of us would be more or less ashamed.

SHAME AND THE ORGANIZATIONAL FORMS OF THE SENSE OF SELF

I believe the foregoing provides support for a Jungian perspective on shame as an emotion that is archetypally inherent in the human being. Yet what role shame plays in a given person's life depends largely on that individual's self-image or self-representation. In other words, the particular story of each person's experience of shame is closely bound up with the development of his self-esteem. In the biblical myth of Paradise, shame arises for the first time in connection with a growing consciousness. This dawning awareness concerns the separation of the self from others (Eve) and from God, and it results in the loss of Paradise and original wholeness.

In some respects this mythical event can be compared with certain features of that phase of childhood development that the infant researcher Daniel Stern called "verbal sense of self," during which the child's first crisis in self-understanding occurs (15–18 months). At this point, the child is able to recognize itself in the mirror – it has developed a rudimentary capacity for making itself into an object. Thus, an "objective self" has been born that stands against the merely "subjective self" of earlier phases. For the first time, the child experiences itself as divided in two and "mourns" the indivisibility of its former experience (loss of Paradise). The capacity to experience shame thus first appears in connection with the realization that the self can also been seen from the outside. One's "subjective" self now begins to make a picture of itself, as it were, and to develop an attitude – if only rudimentary – toward it. Children at this stage refer to themselves in the third person, often applying the same judgments to themselves that they have heard from significant others. For example, one hears a boy say about himself, "Johnny is good" or "Johnny is bad." If Johnny happens to be "bad," he may throw away a toy representing "Johnny," because what is bad deserves to be rejected. Here one can observe the origins of that phenomenon whereby we treat ourselves the same way that our significant others treated us in childhood.

But while a rudimentary consciousness of shame cannot appear before the phase of the verbal self, the origins of shame lie in the "subjective" self developed earlier, as Tomkins was probably correct in assuming. The way we experienced significant others tending to the needs of our infant bodies even influences us at the level of the "core self." This, more than whether we look like movie stars, may determine how comfortable we feel with our bodies. On the other extreme, we may be so ashamed of our bodies that we can hardly even live with or in them. It is commonly known that shame about the body-self is often linked with emotional disorders.

Susceptibility to shame is very common on the level of the "subjective sense of self," with its need for mutuality. Earlier in my discussion of Tomkins's hypothesis, I noted that shame tends to appear when our need for soul connection is not sufficiently met and we are abandoned along with our feelings, thoughts and intuitions. Finding no echo or mirror, we do not feel understood or valued. As a result, we may be ashamed to have had any needs for mutuality or connection in the first place, and resolve to keep these to ourselves in the future. Shame-anxiety of this sort that extends over a period of time contributes to "narcissistic vulnerability." This lends credence to the hypothesis proposed by various writers that narcissistic persons did not have their early intersubjective needs met with sufficient empathy; they felt emotionally abandoned (Kohut 1971a, 1977; Asper 1993).

Feelings of shame can even be observed in the domain of the "emergent sense of self."[3] I think for example of people who have difficulty with learning, who lack the patience to complete each step of a process. They are ashamed of being beginners, of not knowing everything. Like the Goddess Athena springing fully armed from the head of Zeus, they expect their skills to be fully developed from the word go. Of course, one often discerns the demands of the grandiose self in such expectations, but it is also possible that they spring from impatience and exaggerated demands on the part of significant others early in life.

The organizational forms of the sense of self described by Stern, each one "born" at a turning point of early childhood development, determine the basic elements of one's self-understanding. As mentioned, this self-understanding depends on early relational patterns, especially on the expectations, images, and feelings that these interactions left in the unconscious. Fantasies about how I as a person am experienced and seen by others play a decisive role with respect to shame. Many adults suffer from a discrepancy between such fantasies – shaped by interactions with the figures of early childhood – and actual reality. In the case of neurotic shame problems, fantasies of being ashamed usually do not correspond to present reality. This discrepancy often shows up in the transferences stimulated by the psychotherapeutic process. I will have more to say about this in a later chapter.

The quality of care that an infant receives depends, naturally, on the psychic potential and "personal equation" of its parents. It is highly unlikely that harmony would prevail in all areas – nor would it be conducive to the growth of the child's independence. Usually there are certain areas where child and caretaker match, while a subtle lack of empathy may characterize others. The result may be that the child tends to be self-confident in some areas – let's say in the domain of the core-self and its bodily feelings – while inhibition and susceptibility to shame limit him in others – say the domain of psychic and emotional connection. Often, the verbal, rational sphere is emphasized at the cost of spontaneity in the realm of the body and instincts, or that of intuition. Determining the extent to which this represents a development of natural talent, or the fulfillment of parental preferences would require a thorough analysis. However, we do know that shortcomings in one area are often compensated by strengths in another. A basic sense of being "unloved" in all spheres causes an underlying feeling of being utterly rejected, and this condition is accompanied by intense susceptibility to shame. This prepares the ground for severe pathologies of every kind, from completely asocial to destructively addictive behavior. Some persons may seek refuge from these feelings of worthlessness by committing themselves to grand programs requiring personal sacrifice. This socially sanctioned reaction–formation may become an exaggerated, addictive need to help in which a person feels that, "the only way to get rid of my shameful unworthiness is to sacrifice myself for the sake of others." Though such an attitude may coincide with highly esteemed Christian virtues, a problem arises with the urgency of the helper's need to help. Ironically, in these cases the person being helped actually helps the helper – by providing a way for him to overcome his or her feelings of shameful unworthiness (Schmidbauer 1977). Helpers are dependent on those they help, without whom they would fall into the bottomless abyss of their sense of worthlessness and meaninglessness. And this can turn their willingness to help into its opposite.

THE PSYCHOANALYTICAL THEORY OF SHAME: ERIK ERIKSON

At last we turn to the classic theory of shame and its early development set forth by Erik Erikson (1950). Erikson observed a close connection between the origin of shame and the child's realization of its upright and exposed position. This realization takes place during what psychoanalysis has described as the "anal" phase of development – because of its correlation with the maturation of the sphincter muscles. Learning to "let go of" and "hold on to" the feces sets the stage for experimentation with two corresponding sets of social modalities. At the same time, the child begins to "stand on its own two feet," and thus enters a new world of experiences. Thus Erikson viewed the most essential aspect of this phase as a polarity of "autonomy versus shame and doubt" (1950: 251ff). Naturally it is the task of the caretaker to support the child's steps toward autonomy whenever possible, as well as to protect it from meaningless and arbitrary experiences of shame and doubt.

This polarity involves a potential danger, to which Erikson rightly alludes. If the child is denied the gradual experience of increasing autonomy and free choice, it will turn against itself all its urges to discriminate and to manipulate. It will develop a precocious conscience,[4] a tendency to over-manipulate itself. Instead of taking possession of the world of objects and experimenting with them, the child will concentrate compulsively on its own bodily functions.

At this stage, the child also realizes that it has a front and a back side. The backside of the body, the "behind," and all the sensations localized within it, are out of sight for the child and subject to the will of others. Thus, these areas often give rise to feelings of shame and self-doubt, which Erikson graphically described as follows:

> The "behind" is the small being's dark continent, an area of the body which can be magically dominated and effectively invaded by those who would attack one's power of autonomy and who would designate as evil those products of the bowels which were felt to be all right when they were being passed.
>
> (Erikson 1950: 253)

Erikson refers here to a fantasy that can greatly torment persons prone to shame. It has to do with a shameful brooding over what one has "given away" of oneself to others in an uncontrolled way, or with doubts about what one has "left behind." Such doubts often lead to compulsively controlling behavior. I think, for instance, of persons who are never sure if they have left things in order when they leave home – if they really turned off the stove or locked the door. Sometimes such compulsive symptoms are accompanied by high susceptibility to shame, but not always. I may fear that I have said embarrassing and shameful things I wasn't aware of, or otherwise made a bad impression. Then I feel compelled to review every word and interaction searching for suspicious overtones. If I could, I would try to rule out all such possibilities by asking those concerned whether we are still on good terms and thus to reassure myself that I really have not made a bad impression. But once again, shame usually prevents me from doing so.

Erikson's view confirms the decisive importance of interactions with caretakers in this phase, in determining the relationship that will develop later between love and hate, collaboration and stubbornness, freedom for self-actuality and its denial.

> From a sense of self-control without loss of self-esteem comes a lasting sense of good will and pride; from a sense of loss of self-

control and of foreign overcontrol comes a lasting propensity for
doubt and shame.

(Erikson 1950: 254)

The child in this phase is particularly susceptible to being ashamed –
whether this is the result of a deliberate method of child-rearing or
unempathic thoughtlessness. The child's growing perception of its small-
ness is already a blow to its self-confidence. The feeling of being small first
develops when the child learns to stand and begins to become aware of
how relative are the measures of size and power.

In Erikson's view, shame is connected with being seen by others, and is
therefore prior to a sense of guilt, in which one is alone with the voice of the
superego or the internalized "other." One who is ashamed is exposed to
the eyes of the world, as in shame-dreams in which the dreamer finds
himself not completely clothed, or wearing his pajamas in public, or
caught "with his pants down."

Erikson put forth the remarkable thesis that shame – the impulse to hide
one's face or sink into the ground – actually expresses rage, although that
rage is turned against the self. Someone filled with shame would like to
force the world to look away in order to keep his shameful situation from
being seen. If he could, he would put out the condemning eyes of the
world, but short of that, he can only wish to become invisible. Thus, a
person who has been overly shamed may have a secret determination to
get away with things, but he may also exhibit a defiant shamelessness.
Such reaction-formations against susceptibility to shame should not
escape the eye of the psychotherapist.

In many respects, Erikson stands here on the firm ground of psychoanalytic drive-theory, which views shame as a reaction-formation to
exhibitionistic drives (Freud 1965, Jacobson 1964). According to this
theory, feelings of shame manifest themselves whenever conscience
prohibits the urgent desire to show oneself. In such cases, feelings of
shame rather than pleasure and desire accompany sexual activity, although
a certain amount of excitement accompanying the shame suggests an
underlying exhibitionistic impulse. In response to the intrusive twinge of
conscience, one feels suddenly ashamed of wanting to show something off
– whether that something is of a sexual or generally narcissistic nature.

At times, conscience can be the voice of strict prohibitions, stemming
from childhood, that still exercise a sanctioning effect. Exhibitionistic
impulses feel dangerous because they have an aggressive, competitive
quality that can provoke in others a desire for revenge. It is possible to
make others feel ashamed and envious by drawing attention to one's
income or by showing off one's expensive sports car. There are persons
who feel ashamed every time they stand up for something they believe in,
assert themselves, or desire to stand in the limelight (Miller 1985: 33).

In many respects, the Eriksonian interpretation described above seems convincing enough. It is based on what has become the "classical" psychoanalytic view of the instinctual drives that underlie our basic attitudes and social behaviors. On the other hand, a holistic psychology, emphasizing the self and its development, places exhibitionistic wishes and their suppression within the framework of the entire personality. In this view, both self-display and the desire to be seen, and curiosity and the desire to see, are fundamental to our physical, psychic, and social being. They can be described as archetypal patterns of experience and behavior. As such, they are connected to the sexual sphere but not limited to it. Kohut saw the infant's and small child's "narcissistic-exhibitionistic" needs as crucial for the development of the self – and stressed that the mother should accept these needs with empathy and joy.

At the same time, Kohut writes, "optimal frustration" is necessary for the gradual establishment of boundaries and an acceptance of reality and its limits (Kohut 1977: 123ff). I would add that feelings of shame act as "guardians" of these limits – making themselves uncomfortably known whenever these limits are overstepped. But, as mentioned earlier, these limits must be flexible rather than narrow and rigid in order for a person to achieve self-realization.

The neurotic inhibition of aggression sometimes stems from a fear of retribution or punishment. But if such inhibition is experienced more as shame-anxiety, it may be connected to the fear of disapproval. One runs the risk of appearing obtrusive and of being rejected whenever one asks for attention or claims space for oneself. And if one suffers from a lack of self-esteem, even the smallest hint of rejection causes hurt and pain.

The socialization of a child involves setting limits on the "naked truth" of its fantasies and needs, and especially curbing its impulses to immediately act out such needs. Limits are necessary if we want to live in human society. Yet they may also have a stunting effect, furthering neurotic inhibition and suppressing vital, spontaneous expression. As far as society is concerned, the individual requires a "fig leaf" that more or less covers his "naked" inner thoughts, feelings, and impulses. Thus, the development of a "soul-mask" or persona (Jung) is crucial to the individual's relation to society, but it can also result in serious defects.

"FIG LEAF" AND "SOUL MASK"

Let us consider again the loincloth made of fig leaves that Adam and Eve invented in response to their feelings of shame, along with the question, perhaps not so far-fetched, of whether this loincloth could be seen as a primal image of what Jung called the "persona." In dreams, for instance, bodily coverings and clothing are usually interpreted as symbols of the dreamer's "persona attitude." In this context it may be useful to rethink this important Jungian concept – defining the persona as a fig-leaf meant to hide our essential "naked truth," our most intimate core. The persona has therefore the closest possible relationship to shame, whose collective function is to protect us from embarrassing exposure. Jolande Jacobi called the persona the "soul mask" (1971). Unintentionally "letting the mask fall away" because one is overwhelmed by the intoxication of love, alcohol, or rage, for instance, may cause a reaction of shame. This often amounts to a "loss of face."

Persona is the Latin expression for "mask." It is often assumed (Jacobi 1971: 44; Blomeyer 1974) that this term is etymologically related to the verb *personare* which literally means "to sound through." This interpretation draws on the idea that behind ancient theater masks, the voice of the player could be heard with all of its individual nuances, modulations, and vibrations, while the face maintained its fixed features and typical expressions, betraying neither personal happiness nor unhappiness. Unfortunately, such apparently meaningful connections do not seem to be corroborated by etymologists, who deem it unlikely that the noun *persona* (mask) is derived from the verb *personare*. The etymology of the word remains controversial (see *persona* in *Der Kleine Pauly*).

Nevertheless, it is certain that *persona* is the Latin expression for the mask worn by actors in ancient Greek theater. But we need to remember that Greek tragedies always portrayed the figures of myth (Electra, Iphigenia, Antigone, King Agamemnon, Oedipus, etc.) rather than unique individuals engaged in the activities and conflicts of everyday life. In other words, the mask accentuated transpersonal and globally human qualities, while veiling those that were personal and individual. The players grew into the mythical shape expected of them.

Psychologically, the persona is understood to be a mask compatible with a socially accepted "role," a device the individual uses to adapt to his or her environment. To carry out a function in society requires accepting a certain role, and this brings up issues involving self-esteem. Which role do I play in the arena of human social life? Is it an attractive or a hateful role, a main role or only an incidental one? Some roles afford a high degree of narcissistic gratification (and are attended by correspondingly high expectations). Others severely frustrate one's self-esteem. The secret fantasies we may harbor about dream jobs show which roles we find the most attractive. Some persons become one with the role they have assumed and really thrive in it, especially if it is a role that enhances self-worth and dignity. We say then that he or she is a "typical" pastor, diplomat, doctor, university professor, star, teacher or prima donna. All of us have more or less conscious notions about which roles confer the greatest advantages. And we put on masks to hide from other persons (and ourselves) those qualities we find the most disadvantageous.

Although the concept of the persona easily takes on a negative connotation – being judged as morally questionable or hypocritical – Jung wished it to be understood as a value-free term. He saw the persona as vitally necessary for adaptation to the exterior world. It is an innate human response, although what role this response plays within the personality as a whole must be discerned in each case.

It would be impossible to survive our daily lives without the persona, which sums up collective rules of the game in order to relieve us of having to make hundreds of individual decisions. For example, since it is a matter of course to say hello or shake hands when greeting someone, we don't have to think about our approach each and every time. There are conventions at our disposal, yet these need not obscure everything of a personal nature. There are always individual variations in one's tone of voice, the style of one's handshake, and the myriad other expressive signals that regulate closeness and distance. The body language that accompanies conventional interactions is often very eloquent. Still, we need to remember that the persona not only protects our intimacy – by preventing others from reading our innermost thoughts and feelings by the expressions on our faces – it also serves to protect our fellows, whose intimacy we can disrupt through inconsiderate openness. Only "children and fools" tell the truth, since their persona has not developed to the degree expected by society. As adults, we are often required to hide our true thoughts behind social white lies. The same is true of fluctuations in our mood – which are not usually anyone else's business, and indeed tend rather to be a nuisance. To "rejoice with the joyous and weep with the sad" demands a certain consideration of the feelings of those around us. A certain politeness is also required to make life more livable for ourselves and others. In short, we cannot always be completely honest or spontaneous or behave according to how we feel in our innermost hearts. In the course of their socialization, children are taught to develop an adequate persona. Only when they have learned to mask their nakedness behind the appropriate loincloth are they fit to be full members of society. As such, they will have developed a sensibility for how to behave in each situation, without which they would be unwelcome and even ridiculous.

Thus it is essential to give the persona its due place. If it too strongly dominates one's psychic household – consciously or unconsciously – it can stunt one's relation to one's own soul. In this case, what appears to be is confused with what really is; the individual personality rooted in the self is sacrificed to a façade. On the other hand, if the persona is not differentiated enough, one tends to rub others the wrong way. One makes oneself unpopular, and suffers from isolation or feelings of inferiority. It is as if the loincloth did not quite fit or was put together defectively. It feels uncomfortable to wear, and may reveal too much of one's naked intimacy.

Our individual nature is brought into harmony with social needs and expectations only with difficulty, since there exists a fundamental discord between the two. Thus the persona can be nothing more than a "compromise between individual and society as to 'what a man should appear to be'" (Jung 1928: para. 246). And a compromise easily takes on the tinge of something suspicious, if not morally offensive.

According to Jolande Jacobi, a persona that functions well must work toward the harmonious collaboration of three factors:

> First, an ego-ideal consisting of what one would like to be, how one would like to appear; second, the ideal and expectations of one's surroundings, by which one would like to be seen and accepted in a particular way; and third, one's physical and psychic constitution.
>
> (Jacobi 1971: 54)

All of us are familiar with the desire to present the best possible ego ideal or fantasy image of ourselves to those around us. We may do so either in an unrefined or a subtle way. In either case, there is always the risk of mistaking the mask for one's real face. We quickly react with shame if something that does not fit this ideal self-image protrudes from behind the mask. It is a truism to remark about the uneasy relation between the ideal self and the real self, with its attendant shadow areas. In other words, we feel ashamed of our shadow parts.

In order to live up to the expectations of those around us, we must develop a sense of the roles we have been assigned – not all of them immediately obvious. As I have said, starting in early childhood, ideas or representations develop based on patterns of interaction with significant others. These are usually incorporated (often unconsciously) into our inner worlds very early on, and so it is often difficult to differentiate between our own expectations of ourselves and those placed upon us by others. The tendency to project internalized expectations associated with figures from childhood onto persons in our present-day environment is strong. This creates a discrepancy between the expectations that are shaped by our own ideas, and the real expectations of our surroundings. People who move upward socially or who move from the country to the city often suffer from this problem. Insecurity about the expectations of a given environment often produces a shame-anxiety of behaving out of line. In general, social inhibition hides a fear that initiative and spontaneity might seem out of place and cause embarrassment – though often enough this is not the case. However, this does not mean that "tablets" of collective expectations, which assign the individual a professional role and a limited margin of personal freedom, are always illusory and out of line with reality. Pastors, professors, or politicians exposed to the public eye really may not be able to afford certain "human weaknesses" unless they are carried out secretly. By the same token, bourgeois comfort does not fit very well with our image of an artist, and eccentric behavior is assumed of a diva of film or stage.

The third of the factors Jacobi says is essential for a functioning persona is consideration of psychic and physical constitution. Staying with the biblical imagery, we might say that we hide our personal nature behind a fig leaf, and it is important that the "loincloth" befit our particular constitution. This assumes a certain consciousness of each of our psychic and bodily givens, that is, of a certain amount of self-knowledge and self-criticism. When one's individual psyche and physique are not taken into consideration, one's persona attitude smacks of inauthenticity. Usually, this is noticed by others. An impression develops that such persons do not behave according to who they really are; they play a role that they can not really live up to. They want to portray a stereotype from their fantasy that is at odds with their true inner nature. In the parlance of the theater, one might say such a person has been miscast.

Even superficial social transactions should not completely suppress our actual natures. Otherwise, we react from the "False Self" (Winnicott) and are restricted to the limited expressive capacity of our masks. We live only with reference to what others expect from us.

Jacobi held the view that the persona normally only begins to develop in puberty (1971: 57). If a child has a noticeable persona, this is either mere playful imitation of adults or else "a neurotic straight-jacket that oppresses a child that has been too good and too well brought up" (1971: 57). With Blomeyer (1974: 22ff.), I am of the opinion that the persona in puberty goes through additional gender- and phase-specific articulations, but that its roots reach back into earliest childhood.

At this point we have to ask whether Jung, in choosing the metaphor of a mask to represent the function of adaptation to the exterior world, really chose well. Because of Jung's metaphor, the persona's function is usually understood to mean only those modes of behavior that are compatible with public or social roles. We therefore are justified in feeling a certain contempt for those who can never take off their persona masks, even in close relationships. Nevertheless, we always do play a role in our social network, whether that role is lover, spouse, mother, father, friend, teacher, therapist, patient, or student. The essential question is whether we can give to these roles the stamp of our unique individuality and reserve our collective masks for moments of necessity. In spite of its limitations, a role provides a generally recognized framework that in no way completely eliminates personal and intimate interactions. Role confusion always causes difficulties in relationships, for example when a partner acts like a therapist, a mother acts like her son's lover, or a daughter becomes her father's spouse in her fantasy. Even in our most private relationships, we cannot step out of our roles completely. On the other hand, we are fundamentally capable of shaping our roles in a genuinely individual manner, so that we are not forced to hide behind a collective mask when it is not appropriate.

PERSONA (C.G. JUNG) AND
FALSE SELF (D.W. WINNICOTT)

Development of the persona is one part of the process of socialization that occurs in childhood. Thus it would be interesting to ask to what extent Jung's concept of the persona overlaps with Winnicott's concept of the False Self (1960). According to Winnicott, the False Self develops when the maternal caretaker is not sufficiently able to sense or respond to the needs of the infant. The infant is then forced to attune itself to the mother's "gestures" and to adapt itself to her much too early.

> Through this False Self the infant builds up a false set of relationships, and by means of introjections even attains a show of being real, so that the child may grow to be just like mother, nurse, aunt, brother, or whoever at the time dominates the scene.
>
> (Winnicott 1960: 146)

At the same time, the False Self performs a function of great value and importance. By submitting to the demands of the environment, it protects the True Self and guards it from injury.

Winnicott proposed an entire range of different forms in which the False Self expresses itself. On one end of the scale, the False Self behaves pathologically, having completely divorced itself from the True Self's "spontaneous gesture," and thus provokes a feeling of inner emptiness. Winnicott located the healthy individual at the other end of the scale. His reflections on the True and False Self are highly relevant to our topic:

> There is a compliant aspect to the True Self in healthy living, an ability of the infant to comply and not to be exposed. The ability to compromise is an achievement. The equivalent of the False Self in normal development is that which can develop in the child into a social manner, something which is adaptable. In health this social manner represents a compromise.
>
> (Winnicott 1960: 149–50)

Here Winnicott adds the following decisive qualification:

> At the same time, in health, the compromise ceases to become allowable when the issues become crucial. When this happens the True Self is able to override the compliant self.
>
> (Winnicott 1960: 150)

Both Jung and Winnicott emphasize the compromises involved in social behavior, although the persona is not identical with the False Self. The latter simply describes an adaptive submission aimed at protecting the True Self, which results in a severe limitation of spontaneity. The concept of the False Self is thus primarily used in a pathological sense. Winnicott speaks of its equivalent in a healthy person as a "social manner" that is flexible. In Jung's view, the persona in itself is not at all pathological. It only becomes so when the ego is completely identified with it, thus becoming cut off from the soul and its creative vitality. However, I think it is important to emphasize that the antecedents of such persona-identification in the individual's life-history are usually quite similar to those of the False Self. For the therapist, this means that it takes more than good advice or moralizing to deconstruct persona-identification. It may require a deep analysis of childhood wounds.

Shame stands in close relationship to the persona. When the persona has holes in it, letting what is beneath "show through," there is a feeling of nakedness, and thus a reaction of shame. We must repeatedly emphasize that great care must be taken to prevent the persona from cutting us off from our genuine, basic nature. The sense of basic nature is what allows us to remain more or less "ourselves" or at least to come back to ourselves after a temporary departure, caused for instance by our craving to be admired. It is also this sense that makes us self-critically aware when our persona begins to operate "autonomously" and out of control – for example, when we boast of having knowledge that we haven't really mastered, or seek the limelight in some other way. Shame lets us know that we are acting out our needs for admiration inappropriately. We may feel even more ashamed to have this arrogance pointed out to us by others. The persona asks the questions: what do others think of me? In what light am I seen? Will others take me seriously and respect me as a person? Do I fall too far outside of the "norm"? If so, do people marvel at me for being so far above average or laugh at me for being ridiculously out of place? For example, a woman who wears an "outrageous" dress that suits her particularly well will win admiration and inspire others to imitate her. But if she tries too hard to be "unusual," and wears a dress that does not suit her, she will be the target of deprecating comments. "Outrageous" ideas of every sort can meet with the same fate.

In my practice, I have repeatedly noticed how closely issues concerning clothing are bound up with self-esteem. Sometimes, especially among women, this becomes very problematic. Symbolically, clothing represents the persona. Clothing in dreams usually addresses this theme, eloquently expressing how we see ourselves and want to be seen by others, how we "dress" ourselves to establish our validity, or fail to do so. One must not only be ashamed of unprotected, naked openness. We may also be exposed to danger when our veils are found to be inappropriate. The persona may provide people who are vulnerable and susceptible to shame with something to hide behind. But it may also be exposed as a masquerade. In any case, the protection is only relative, since identification with the persona can never replace realistic self-esteem.

5

VARIATIONS ON THE EXPERIENCE OF SHAME

THE INFERIORITY COMPLEX

The so-called inferiority complex is very closely related to shame-anxiety. Thus it would be worth our while to give some thought to this notion, which has become part of our everyday language. It is based on the idea that certain parts of one's personality are of inferior value (I may feel that I am ugly, unintelligent, untalented, small, fat, unpopular, etc.). Such ideas are accompanied by strong feelings of dissatisfaction with oneself, even to the point of self-hatred. Envy and jealousy also play their part. We are envious of all those to whom fate seems to have given a better lot. We feel compelled to compare ourselves with others, especially those whom we view as vastly superior to us. These people seem to look down on us disparagingly, provoking highly unpleasant feelings of shame. In order to escape from such debilitating feelings, as well as envy and jealousy, a person often employs the defense mechanism of idealization. If I place others on a pedestal where they appear stylized and out of reach, I can accept their superiority. I can admire them, since their uniqueness places them outside the area of a fantasized or actual rivalry. For persons with serious inferiority complexes, open rivalry is often linked with shame. To engage in any sort of competition might reveal one's presumptuous overestimation of oneself; thus, feelings of rivalry are usually cloaked in shame. But what would it take for us to get over the embarrassing feeling of inferiority? For the most part, only unsatisfying or unrealistic remedies occur to us. For example, we think, "If only I were not so inhibited, if only I were smarter, more attractive, intelligent, slimmer. If only I didn't have such an ugly nose or bad skin." Beneath these wishes for improvement there usually lies an ideal fantasy image of oneself, the whole of which is not so easily apprehended. What we experience directly is only the embarrassing discrepancy between the fantasy image we would like to fulfill and our sense of inadequacy in the face of it. Sometimes this fantasy image becomes visible through projections. Idealization is not always just a defense; sometimes we project

61

our ego ideal onto others in the hopes of somehow "getting into their skins," or at least becoming like them.

Who sets the standard by which I measure my worth or lack of worth? When one is in a state of inferiority, one grants this standard unquestioned validity, obediently accepting it as a definitive, authoritative judge. But in my opinion, this judge itself needs to be examined; unquestioned standards are usually the result of patterns of relationship internalized in childhood. As we will observe later, one task of psychotherapy is to re-evaluate this valuing/devaluing authority. Much freedom may be gained by discovering the unconscious ties between this authority and the value systems embodied by significant others from one's past.

In many cases this judgmental authority corresponds not only to the internalized value system of one's parents but to the grandiose self as well. This is especially so when a certain perfectionism predominates, giving one the feeling, "Whatever I am, whatever I can accomplish, is never good enough." The quest for perfection becomes one's most consuming preoccupation, though this aspiration is aborted at the slightest disappointment. Any appearance of deficiency becomes a cause for shame, plunging one into an abyss of humiliation and self-loathing. At the same time, one is ashamed of even having the grandiose expectation of being able to achieve something perfect in the first place.

Here we might stop and ask whether the impossible demands of the inner judge are always at the root of the inferiority complex. Could it not also be an awareness of one's real inadequacy, a self-consciousness that could prompt one to undertake helpful learning programs? What is the difference between an inferiority complex and the realization of one's "actual" inferiority, either of which can cause shame? In other words, what is the criterion by which we judge?

The analytical psychology of Jung holds that the criterion (from the Greek *krites*, judge) resides finally within each of us. If we learn to listen closely, we can make out something like a "voice" of the inner Self and develop a sensitivity for what "sounds" right for us. This personal voice may not speak loudly and may become audible only after significant "trial and error."

Practically speaking, it is best to consider various interpretations of our feelings of inferiority, and to take dreams into account should they arise. Then we may discover that our perception of the inferiority of certain parts of ourselves may be accurate. Whether our imperfections result in an actual inferiority complex depends on the attitude that we take toward our inadequacies, and whether specific shortcomings – of mind, body, character – result in a global negative self-estimation.

One of the characteristics of a complex is that it acts like a magnet, attracting large portions of psychic experience into its field, bending them to its "power" (Jung 1939; Jacobi 1959; Kast 1980). In other words, we not only perceive our limits and inadequacies with great pain, trying to improve, work on, or reconcile ourselves to such deficiencies; in addition, the perception of a certain defect can affect our whole underlying mood. We must also consider the possibility that persons whose underlying mood is one of self-torment will seek out real personality defects in themselves in order to justify their feeling of complete inferiority. Complexes have archaic roots. Thus, when they begin to dominate experience they convey a feeling of all or nothing. The perception of certain specific inadequacies then snowballs into a conviction of one's complete inferiority – a fertile ground for susceptibility to shame.

It is common knowledge that C.G. Jung worked out a typology of attitudes (extraversion and introversion) and functions of consciousness (thinking, feeling, intuition, and sensation) (Jung 1921). He came to the conclusion that we require all of these attitudes and functions in order to deal with life, but that we can never develop them all to the same extent. We develop most the function that most closely corresponds to our natural talents, the so-called "principal" or "main" function, along with a secondary or "auxiliary" function. Jung described the function that remained most undeveloped and undifferentiated the "inferior" function.

We cannot explore here the extent to which Jung's theory of the types is still defensible, yet it is the concept of the inferior function that I find to be relevant in the present connection. By means of this concept, inadequate or inferior behavior is limited to a circumscribed psychic province. For example, if I know that thinking is my inferior function, I may have to live with the knowledge that razor-sharp logic is not my strength, that I always lose at chess, and that I feel dumb and ashamed at the computer. My principal function, accordingly, would be feeling, and my strength would lie in assessing things in a differentiated way and in being able to judge and weigh both sides of a matter. And I would probably have a particular talent for empathy as well.

In partnerships, the following dynamic can sometimes be observed: partner A feels at a disadvantage around partner B because the former always clings to observable facts and concrete things, while his friend, B, seems to readily grasp people's underlying, hidden dimensions, their ideas, motivations, and ways of acting. But then partner B has marked difficulty orienting himself in the here and now, organizing his time and bringing order into his life. He tends to delegate these functions to partner A since they are his strength. Here partner A is dealing with the "inferior" sensation function on the part of partner B, while partner A is able to employ his sensation in a differentiated way. Partner B's principal function is intuition.

This stereotyped vignette should suffice as an example of how the inferior function works. What I would like to emphasize here is that weaknesses and inadequacies can be seen as involving limited parts of the personality. This does not mean that the inferior function cannot get one into really shameful situations, or that one can escape from suffering from its lashings. Nor does it prevent some Jungians from abusing the theory, making their inferior functions the cheapest possible excuse for tactlessness, undependability, or stupidity.

The inferior function can easily degenerate into an inferiority complex, to which self-esteem soon falls prey. For example, I think of a young Swiss woman who suffered from a profound disturbance of self-worth. This disturbance was caused by, among other things, the fact that she was an unusually introverted, intuitive person who lived in a world of premonitions, fantasies, and images. Due to her correspondingly "inferior" sensation function, it was difficult for this young woman to take care of her household in a very exacting manner. She simply did not notice every single fleck of dust on the furniture and, therefore, simply did not remove it. Now in a real Swiss family, a perfectly clean household is a matter of the greatest importance. If visitors should come away with the impression that one's house is a pigsty, one would be overcome with degrading shame. Such a collective attitude made life difficult for my patient from an early age on. She was called a "dumb goose" who couldn't even see the dust on the furniture; in her stupidity, it was said, she would never find a husband. These same people criticized her extraordinary fantasy life and capacity for contemplative depths as dreaminess and otherworldliness. It is no wonder she later suffered from destructive self-rejection, a huge inferiority complex, and tormenting feelings of shame.

Parental figures who give priority to modes of behavior that happen to be the child's inferior function – and devalue its differentiated function – cause difficulties for the child in its search for identity. An academically oriented family, for instance, may not prize refined and differentiated feelings. They may also fail to recognize the value of a talent for "sensation," a function oriented toward practical matters. Rather, they will most likely be committed to a belief in the supremacy of academic achievements and thinking.

The inferiority complex is linked with a strong susceptibility to shame. Alfred Adler, who originally coined the term, assumed that desperate eagerness to achieve personal importance (*Geltungsstreben*, *Geltungssucht*) should be viewed as an "over-compensation," a reaction-formation against the endless shame one feels about one's supposed inferiority. In the terminology of modern narcissism theory, this would be the equivalent of an identification with the grandiose self, which shows itself as "narcissistic grandiosity." Of course this overblown grandiosity threatens to collapse like a house of cards at the slightest insult. One way of denying the deep abyss of shame that lies within is to fly off in a rage at the audacity of anyone who dares call my grandiosity into question. However, in an "hour of truth," we may feel a sense of shame that signals to us that we have deviated from the "plain" truth, as Aristotle put it. In other words, we can become aware of our inflations. And once a mirror has been held up to them, we may be ashamed of our exaggerated, illusory wishes – perhaps in a healthy way.

Another way to escape one's inferiority complex and the danger of constant shame is to withdraw from human contact, to hide behind a sort of persona, a mask that seems cold and removed. Many people who suffer from this problem are simply amazed to learn that others find them proud and condescending and that this is the source of their unpopularity. It seems so foreign to their own subjective experience of inferiority and fear of shame. They find themselves in a vicious circle, in a psychological pattern that goes something like this: "I have to protect myself from the possibility that others will see my true lack of worth, for this would cast me into a bottomless pit of shame. I would be written off, blacklisted, and despised for the rest of my life. Since this fear of shame forces me to avoid contact as much as possible, I become isolated from other persons. Apparently no one wants to have anything to do with me, which in turn confirms the low opinion I have of myself. And the more inferior I feel, the more I want to avoid being seen by others." An extended course of psychotherapy would be required to modify such a vicious circle.

In contrast to this state of affairs are those who peddle their inferiority complexes, telling everyone about their weaknesses, whether they want to hear about them or not. This is another form of defense born of inner distress. It carries with it the hope that one will be appreciated for this very self-criticism. Whatever the case, beneath such behavior usually lies the largely unconscious intention of revealing one's sore spots in order to prevent others from doing so and thereby causing one shame. The goal here is to maintain control. By demonstrating an awareness of one's own weaknesses, one deprives others of any opportunity for attack.

It is not far from this behavior to another form of defense prompted by the inferiority complex: the need for constant self-control and self-surveillance in order to prevent oneself from being seen warts and all.

Of course, social life would be inconceivable without self-restraint, as would growth in consciousness – which is based largely on self-observation. After all, psychotherapy and analysis presuppose an ability to direct one's attention to the self and to whatever transpires within it. But we must distinguish such self-awareness from the compulsion to watch oneself incessantly. Excessive self-surveillance blocks all spontaneity, replacing it with various forms of inhibition that become the target of further condemnation by the "inner eye." Although we may try to compensate with brashness, most of the time such inhibition only sends us into an escalating spiral. Compulsive self-surveillance causes inhibition; inhibition causes shame, and the resulting intensified self-observation causes yet more inhibition.

To recapitulate, the capacity for self-observation comes into being at the age of about 18 months, as the phase of the "verbal self" is developing. It coincides with the realization that one's own self can also be seen from the outside, as others see it. It is significant that persons who are caught in an inferiority complex and feel compelled to constantly monitor themselves have an "inner eye" that is invariably intolerant, critical, and intensely demeaning. Thus, the self is devalued from the inside, while at the same time being exposed to the observations of others, which one imagines as harsh and disapproving. It is as if one is forced to constantly regard oneself from the outside.

A musician began analysis because he suffered from a bad case of stage fright, which severely impaired his technique and expressive ability. The problem was mortifying to him. Closer analysis revealed that as soon as he stepped on stage he became consumed by thoughts about what impression he was making on the audience, how his playing was being received, how his performance was being judged. This made it impossible to stay "with himself" and greatly disturbed his concentration on the interpretation of the musical work. Naturally his self-observation (which he imagined as coming from the audience) was merciless, and the slightest unevenness in his performance made him want to sink through the floor in shame. The more embarrassed he became, the more inhibited was his playing, and the more compelling his nightmarish image of his failure. Eventually, public performances became pure torture. His psychic problem consisted of assigning too much power to an imagined "they," a strict and disapproving audience that intimidated and paralyzed him. He felt a compulsion to imagine others as devaluing, and to belittle himself because of it.

In general, however, critical self-observation is of decisive importance in any achievement. The musical world offers a beautiful example of this from the great cellist, Pablo Casals, who spoke of the *dédoublement*, which must take place the entire time a musician is performing.

> Abandoned to the music in self-forgetfulness, yet he remains attentive and in possession of his self, staying constantly relaxed at his instrument, working economically and without forced effort, in order not to disturb or inhibit his musical expression.
>
> (Tobel 1945: 30ff)

Casals goes on to describe the musician's attentive self-control in which he imagines his audience's expectation of a profound musical experience. In contrast to my analysand, however, Casals seems to have been sufficiently confident that he could actually fulfill such expectations.

In general, compulsive self-observation becomes a problem only when others are present. Seeing ourselves as if through the eyes of others, we lose access to our own spontaneous wellsprings. We feel unremittingly exposed to the looks of others, whom we imagine as critical and derogatory. For example, a young man who suffered from an inferiority complex kept complaining to me about how he assigned others too much importance, and how he oriented himself too much according to what others thought about him. This made him unsure of himself. It took some time for him to realize that these "others" were projections of his own disapproving attitude toward himself.

I hope that in the foregoing I have raised some relevant viewpoints on the inner dynamics of the inferiority complex and its relationship to shame.

EMBARRASSMENT AND SHAME-DESIRE

We now turn to shame reactions that are not necessarily based on an inferiority complex, but rather on behavior beyond one's control, things "that could happen to anyone" and that result in the transgression of some boundary of shame. I am speaking of situations that are embarrassing. Shame reactions in these cases are usually only temporary, having been brought on when parts of oneself that are "nobody's business" suddenly and unintentionally become quite visible. Excitement or zeal may allow something to slip out by mistake that would have stayed in check if sobriety has prevailed. For example, a man might make a critical one-sided remark about the work of a successful colleague. Later, he realizes that the remark was motivated in part by envy, which makes him feel awkward and embarrassed. He now wishes he had tempered his criticism with some humorous, casual comment such as, "You wouldn't happen to detect a note of 'sour grapes' in my voice, would you?" By doing so, he would have apprised his listeners of his envy, while at the same time minimizing its importance, by at least demonstrating his awareness of it. Now every time he thinks of those three persons who heard his criticism, an "embarrassing" and shameful feeling creeps over him – for in their eyes, he is a jealous man. The situation leaves him no choice but to summon tolerance for this shadow part of himself, and to accept the fact that others have seen it.

The more rigid and narrow are our boundaries of shame, the more they restrict our freedom and spontaneity, the greater is the likelihood that repressed contents will slip out of the unconscious. I think for example of an extremely distinguished lady who felt obliged to immediately clean up every crumb that her charming and jovial husband let fall on the table whenever the two of them went for a visit. Apparently she was extremely embarrassed by her husband's "messiness" in the presence of her hosts. Then one evening at the close of one of these visits, a mishap occurred that caused her unspeakable embarrassment. As she was leaving, she lifted her spotless white handbag, which made an unanticipated twist in mid-air and tipped over a bottle half-full of red wine. The bottle's contents drained mercilessly over the table cloth, her dress, and the host's carpet. Clearly nothing could have been more mortifying to this woman. The host sensed her embarrassment, assuring her that this sort of thing had happened before on more than one occasion and that the carpet would prove sufficiently resistant to wine stains. Still, the woman maintained her upright demeanor with an iron-clad will, and all that she could not hide was a blush.

Despite the poor lady's intense embarrassment, her host could not help laughing in secret. It was as if the unconscious had taken revenge on her for imprisoning her life in such a tight shell, for wrapping herself – and her husband – in shame. For her, the event was a damaging intrusion into the structure of her self-respect. A touch of humor would have been required for her to work through such an embarrassing event, and thus the incident may yet have had some meaning for her. Was the spirit of life at work here causing an "accident" for the sake of greater freedom?

Often, a conflict lies beneath one's feelings of embarrassment. For example, one may secretly wish to show certain aspects of oneself, or at least allow them to be seen. But on the other hand, one is inhibited by the shame-anxiety that one's wish might be understood as a desire for self-revelation or some kind of exhibitionism. For example, one might imagine a pubescent girl whose breasts are obviously beginning to develop. Should she be proud of this change, or find it a source of embarrassment to be noticed in this way? Would she rather be seen or not seen in this state? Or take a boy entering adolescence, who "unintentionally" situates himself in the shower room such that his first pubic hairs are on display for all to see – the sign of a budding masculinity that he is secretly proud of. Of course, at the same time, the desire to show off is embarrassing to him. In both cases, embarrassing ambivalence grows out of his insecurity. How should new developments be evaluated and integrated? How does he appear in the eyes of others?

Whenever the body and sexual attraction are at issue, the archetypal shame of nakedness is involved, even if this is shaped by contemporary attitudes or a particular family climate. In certain child-rearing practices sexual matters and nakedness may be treated openly and honestly, but feelings of shame are nonetheless unavoidable. Especially at adolescence, certain situations invariably trigger blushing, a reaction that often expresses shame mixed with desire. We might call this phenomenon "shame-desire" and attribute to it the titillation one feels in the realm of love and sex. On the one hand, shame may severely dampen the joy of one's love life. On the other, mere lust can violently intrude on the boundaries of shame (rape of all kinds is the most blatant example). But there are many love situations in which the feeling of shame enhances sexual desire. Then again mere lust can become "humanized" when tempered by a certain amount of shame – the urge for immediate gratification of desire can be limited and redirected toward fantasy, feeling, and empathy.

Of course, shame-desire is not restricted to matters of love. It can also emerge when one suddenly finds oneself at the center of attention, showered with compliments at a gathering, or asked to give a speech. These situations may be embarrassing, but they can also afford a certain narcissistic rush if one manages to make the best of them. The embarrassment with which we often react to admiration and praise has the quality of shame-desire: we are both embarrassed and delighted. What is troublesome is that those who observe our reactions may find us to be conceited or narcissistic – a judgment we would prefer to avoid. Those who are used to being admired usually have a more or less ritualized response at the ready, such as, "I'm glad that you weren't displeased" or "It's always a pleasure to receive compliments." Being accustomed to success reduces shame-desire, as well as the narcissistic rush associated with unexpected, enthusiastic affirmation.

Shame-desire thus expresses our ambivalence, a combination of both "yes" and "no." Though I would like to be seen and admired for my beautiful body, glorious income, or prodigious talents, I am also afraid to have this need become too obvious and cause shame. Others might see my joy in exposing myself as embarrassing and misplaced. Sometimes my desirous wish will outweigh my caution, and I will expose myself in spite of my subliminal feelings of shame. Then again, at other times, the shame wins out and I will retreat back into my shell.

Once again, how well I am able to accept all of myself, including my shadow side, is of decisive importance. It is this factor more than any other that determines how intense my fear of being seen by unforgiving eyes or of committing a *faux pas* that makes me seem ridiculous and degraded, will be.

HUMILIATION

Humiliation is felt more acutely than embarrassment or shame-desire. At root, we often discover a violation of or open disdain for one's human dignity by overpowering others. For example, one may have been the victim of physical or emotional rape, in which the rage that ordinarily rises in defense of one's self-respect was stifled. It its place, profound shame sets in. This shame beyond measure is caused by a sense of having been humiliated and defiled. One imagines that others view one with pure contempt superficially disguised as pity. This probably explains why so many women prefer to remain silent about their experiences of rape; they do not care to appear as degraded and defiled victims, to expose themselves to unending shame.

Concentration camp survivors also know the hideous shame of the condemned, of those who have been subjected to unspeakable degradation. Most of them had no choice but to hide their painful humiliation deep within themselves, to split it off from the rest of their personality in order to have the semblance of a normal life. Such dehumanizing traumata may cause lasting emotional damage. But perhaps at least the immeasurable shame it causes can be compensated by the knowledge that – having experienced barbaric persecution – one is in the best of company.

Humiliation revolves around experiences of power and powerlessness. One is brought low or oppressed by those who wield power from above. There may be a loss of autonomy as one is made to be subservient, a kind of slave. Whether such a loss of autonomy and agency is experienced as shameful degradation depends on the extent to which one values one's freedom. Autonomy and free will can also be burdensome responsibilities whose delegation to someone who knows better can be very comfortable for some people's egos. After all, our autonomy is always limited and we are always somewhat dependent, not only on others, but also on the condition of our health, our particular fate, and not lastly, the powers of the unconscious. Thus, we would do well to be open and receptive to these powers and to carefully investigate what they want from us.

Creating a relationship between the ego and the unconscious does not mean that we allow consciousness with its freedom to choose to become a purely passive instrument of the unconscious. C.G. Jung rightly spoke of the ego's "confrontation with the unconscious," and not of blind allegiance to it. He viewed the unconscious as "nature," something beyond good and evil, and therefore demanding our consciousness and alertness. "Man always has some mental reservation, even in the face of divine decrees," wrote Jung. "Otherwise, where would be his freedom? And what would be the use of that freedom if it could not threaten Him who threatens it?" (Jung and Jaffé 1963: 247ff). I find it essential to affirm and support the freedom of ego consciousness over against the unconscious, if possible. We require this freedom in order to deal flexibly with the fantasies and impulses of the unconscious. In his own "confrontation with the unconscious," Jung himself was exemplary for taking this stance. If he had not had the power and determination to recognize and live the overpowering experiences his unconscious was bringing him on the symbolic plane, he might well have become an "artist" (as a certain "anima" figure persistently urged), or worse, a missionary and founder of a sect. But he was able to continually ask what these contents meant for his way of being. He always honored his "mental reservations."

I emphasize this point because it is easy, by idealizing the unconscious, to overlook its perils. So strong is the drive to discover the wisdom of the unconscious, to find fulfillment in life by surrendering to something greater and transpersonal – a need that traditional religions once satisfied – that various sects and their fanatical gurus and dictators hold a definite appeal. Fundamentalism is gaining ground, not only in Islam, but in Christendom, for it allows followers to hold onto the letter of the law, to cling to those who pronounce the truth with unshakable conviction, to claim power and subjugation in its name. In such fundamentalist sects, one gives up freedom and autonomy in exchange for the security of knowing what I can count on. Amidst the potentially fruitful crisis and decline of values our civilization is presently undergoing, such religious or pseudo-religious groups seem to promise salvation. The individual who believes such promises does not feel degraded. Apparently he abdicates his right of critical thinking, his autonomy, and his responsibility without coercion and in the name of a higher ideal. But beneath the surface of this apparent free choice one may detect the seductive allure of programs that prey on a primitive hunger for meaning, a hunger arising out of the unconscious. This is not to say that all groups based on religious or quasi-religious ideas belong in the same category. In my view, it is the degree to which individual members are allowed to freely criticize and question that determines the ethical and spiritual caliber of a group.

Another interesting digression deals with the question of why Christianity is centered on a redeemer who was profoundly degraded – spat upon, flagellated, and nailed to a cross. Has not the Church, in alliance with those in political power, interpreted this to mean that the highest virtue lies in subservience, humility, obedience, and the abdication of autonomous thinking? Have not authorities of church and state pronounced it Christian virtue to carry the cross of poverty and submission, while tracing doubt, questions, and rebellion to the devil, who works not for the sake of divine redemption but eternal damnation? (already on this earth!).These also seem to me fundamentalist ideas – misunderstandings of religious truth that are nevertheless promoted by certain authorities. For on a symbolic plane, the suffering and crucifixion of Christ have a profound meaning, which C.G. Jung, among others, have sought to elucidate in studies in the psychology of religion (Jung 1951). On the other hand, the ideology of humiliation and uncritical obedience did not keep the Christian Occident from destroying heretics and pagans by fire and sword, from enslaving them and brutally robbing them of their human and religious dignity. The problems of the Third World, which seem so insoluble today, are to a great extent the result of such Christian policies of all-knowing superiority.

Returning to the powers of the unconscious, which are finally stronger than the so-called "free" will, I would like to give some thought to the following considerations: as long as energies are flowing to us from the unconscious, energies that are affirmed by ego consciousness and experienced as "ego-syntonic," we feel inspired, in good form, and endowed with power and energy. We only begin to feel shame and degradation when the powers of the unconscious urge us to act against our better will and judgment. This is why neurotic symptoms that limit our free choice, such as intense anxiety or compulsion, have such a shaming effect. And

71

addictions, to which we are repeatedly subjected against our will, can drain us of our self-respect in a most humiliating way. Among alcoholics, for example, the shame that follows excessive drinking often becomes so overwhelming that it has to be washed away with additional doses of alcohol.

But feelings of humiliation and shame may also stem from excessive vulnerability. Harmless remarks or small slights may be experienced as degrading if they hit a vulnerable spot. Some people react to such hurts by taking offense, being enraged, or swearing vengeance. Others, who become conscious of the inappropriateness of their reactions, may even feel more ashamed by the realization that they have made a mountain out of a molehill. Persons who are constantly feeling insulted and humiliated by others are usually not very popular. But it should be remembered that apparently petty matters that are experienced as insulting and demeaning, are often simply reprises of old and real childhood humiliations.

Depth psychologists are not only concerned with conscious feelings of humiliation but with those that are so unbearable they become unconscious. At times, only onlookers seem to be aware that someone is in a degrading situation. The person standing in its midst seems unaware and curiously unaffected. His eyes are opened only with great effort, an effort that is not always ethically justified. For example, radical intellectuals of the late sixties were very concerned to awaken people, especially workers, to the fact that they were being exploited and degraded by the capitalist system. The neutral observer, however, was prompted to ask whether it really was a matter of raising workers' consciousnesses to something they were obviously unconscious of, or rather of fanning the flames of a dissatisfaction that is simply inherent in the human situation, however we may twist and turn it. It is well known that this consciousness-raising was not too successful.

Or, as another example, with certain couples, one wonders whether to point out the fact that one partner unconsciously allows him or herself to be dominated and emotionally exploited by the other. The same is true when one is tempted to wake up the members of certain groups or institutions to the fact that they are being required to act in a slavishly obedient manner. For the person involved, membership in such a group can meet a need for surrender to a higher ideal. And who would presume to determine whether another person is fulfilling a meaningful task in life, or simply abdicating his responsibility, overcompensating at the same time his feelings of shame?

The decisive factor in such cases is whether a person has entered into such obligations freely or made the choice willingly. Of course, the psychology of the unconscious reserves a certain skepticism about the so-called "free will." It asks instead whether there are not unconscious, perhaps destructive motivations pushing the free will, as it were, from behind.

MASOCHISM

All of these matters are even further complicated by the fact that humiliating subjugation is sometimes felt as an intense need, even a sexual pleasure. One may develop a bond to the very persons or groups that have degraded, shamed, and tortured one. Though outsiders – therapists among them – may express outrage, and attempt to liberate the victim from his subservience, all such efforts are condemned to failure as long as the humiliation is a need that is consciously or unconsciously laced with pleasure.

Since the time of Krafft-Ebing (1892), the term "masochism" has been used to describe the desire to put oneself through pain and degradation. The term refers to a sexually stimulating wish to experience torture, bondage, and humiliation as the "slave" of some mistress or brutal taskmaster. Not every form of masochistic behavior manifests on a sexual level, but there is always – often unconsciously – a wish to experience degradation and pain.

Here I would like to refer to an interesting historical document that reveals a great deal about the genesis of sexual masochism, namely, *The Confessions of Jean-Jacques Rousseau*. In it, Rousseau described the floggings he endured at the hand of his governess as a boy – episodes "in which so much sensuality was intermixed with pain and disgrace" that he continually attempted to provoke new beatings.

> Who could have supposed that this childish punishment, received at
> the age of eight at the hands of a woman of thirty, would determine
> my tastes and desires, my passions, my very self of my life, and that
> in a sense diametrically opposed to the one in which they should
> normally have developed.
>
> (Rousseau 1954: 26)

Rousseau reports that later it was as though he were possessed by the wish to project his naked posterior toward girls in order to experience the pleasurable floggings.

We know from Rousseau's biography that his mother died while giving birth to him. "I was born, a poor and sickly child, and cost my mother her life. So my birth was the first of my misfortunes" (Rousseau 1954: 19). His father seems to have suffered intensely from the loss of his wife and thus felt very ambivalent toward his son. On the one hand, he saw his beloved wife in the young Jean-Jacques, but on the other could not forget that it was this very child who had taken her away from him.

Thus it seems plausible that Rousseau's masochism stemmed from unconscious self-punishment aimed at exonerating him from guilt over the death of his mother. By enduring pain and degradation he could, in his fantasy, win back his mother's love. Is it all too speculative to apply this pattern to Rousseau's later works as a writer and thinker? Thus we could say that he provoked his contemporaries by valuing everything that had to do with mother nature far above the achievements of civilization, and generally advocating a back to nature philosophy. "Everything is good as it comes from the hands of the Author of Nature; but everything degenerates in the hands of man" (Rousseau 1926: 1). Apparently he felt loved by "great mother nature," when he took upon himself hatred and humiliation by his contemporaries on her behalf. To please her he showed society his naked bottom, that is, he exposed his extremely personal thoughts and feelings in a very unconventional way in order to position himself for the welcome blows.

Let me add that the neurotic constellation I have described does not in any way devalue the genius of such an influential and innovative thinker as Rousseau. Perhaps unconscious motivations such as these were even necessary to the development and expression of his ideas – ideas that were to be decisive in influencing the outbreak of the French Revolution.

To recap, masochism is a feeling of pleasurable satisfaction that comes about by being tortured or humiliated, whether at the hands of others or oneself. However, the pleasurable element of the suffering is often fended off, repressed, or denied. Every psychotherapist sees clients who, though they have come for help, stubbornly resist every improvement, every decrease in suffering. The underlying masochistic component in such clients may only reveal itself over time, when this resistance leads to a "negative therapeutic reaction."

By way of example, I think of a young woman who communicated the message to her therapist and others she encountered, "Don't look at me; I am so disgusting." She felt ashamed of her existence and neglected her appearance in a quite flagrant way. In therapy, the theme of her ugliness was amplified by the blunt statement, repeated often, "I am so incredibly dumb. I am a stupid ass," and by her constant remark to me, "I know you must despise me." In reality she was neither ugly nor dumb. On the contrary, in spite of her unkempt appearance, she seemed to me to have a great deal of imagination and a hidden, girlish charm. Though I checked, I could find no trace of contempt in myself.

Before long, made wiser by other bad experiences, I realized that I should under no circumstances allow myself to fall in the trap my client had set for me. Above all, I realized, I had better not let her know that in my eyes she was not ugly, revolting, or dumb. On the one hand, she wanted desperately to hear this message from me, and on the other she couldn't bear to hear it. As soon as I hinted anything of the sort, she shot back the accusation that I did not take her seriously, that I was only treating her therapeutically and attempting to comfort her. She really knew that I despised her.

By way of anamnesis, I should add that my patient's mother had been so exhausted physically and psychically at the time of her pregnancy that the child must have seemed like an impossible burden for her. Although the mother apparently attempted to do her best, her care must have been very unreliable and dependent upon her changing moods. But the greatest scar was caused by her zeal to have her child grow up as healthy as possible. To this end she frequently administered enemas for the purpose of ridding the daughter of all that was unhealthy inside her body. The patient experienced each of these procedures as a rape and humiliation and recalled traumatic scenes in which she screamed for her life and tried to run away. In part, she interpreted the enemas as punishment for all that was dirty and bad inside her. Then again it satisfied a certain desire by bringing her disguised sexual attentions of her mother. The entire matter was freighted with shame, and the client had great difficulty talking with me about it.[5]

Aspects of her behavior that fit this pattern could still be observed. When she could subjugate herself to another and confess everything that was disgusting about herself, she was able to feel cared for, even a certain sexualized satisfaction. But when she allowed herself to feel impulses toward autonomy, she felt sinfully proud and greatly feared rejection by her inner mother figure. Thus she was not allowed to feel better or attractive, or in any sense be satisfied with herself. If she did, she felt, she would be abandoned by her inner mother and overwhelmed by all that was bad in her own character.

Though her most immediate appeal to the therapist was for protection against the humiliating shame and torturing self-hatred that plagued her, it eventually became clear that no recovery would be allowed. Her unconscious complex sabotaged any improvement.

In my practice, I have found that those who were subjected to such health regimes as children tend to become subservient to others as adults. Generally, they also mistrust anything that they would like to express, verbally or emotionally, as if they had no right to their own inner life. In analysis, repressed sadistic fantasies and intense rage often surface. Their sexual wishes and fantasies are strongly associated with the anal region.

But even when a person experiences a pleasurable reaction or satisfaction to humiliation, pain, and subjugation, he may still suffer intense shame over his masochism. In sexual masochism, while pleasure is sought by means of pain, whipping, bondage, and enslavement, these perverse wishes may at the same time be invested with shame. Often the person fears that if his perversion became known, he would be disgraced, the target of public censure. Thus masochistic aspirations are restricted to a secluded, intimate sphere. They are rarely ego-syntonic, and one may indeed suffer from a sense of being overpowered by perversions and of not being normal.

Masochism of a more mental and psychosocial nature often requires a rationalization or an idealized goal in order to be permitted by the ego. For example, one subjects oneself to higher goals and ideals, or as described earlier, to persons who embody such goals and ideals in a powerful way. When it comes to transpersonal, religious or political causes, for which great sacrifices are required, it is often difficult to differentiate between a person seeking masochistic satisfaction and one who has truly surrendered his ego. Is it masochistic to go to jail or even undergo tortures for the sake of one's belief in human dignity or in resistance to some dictator's corrupt policies? I don't think so, necessarily, and therefore I believe that one must be careful in using the derogative term "masochistic," restricting it to behavior in which self-torture has become an end in itself (Cf. Gordon 1987).

Of course, not all of the degradations children suffer lead to masochistic behavior. Some lead to "narcissistic rage" – whose sadistic fantasies make it the converse form of reaction, the other side of the coin, so to speak (Kohut 1971b, Jacoby 1990: 171–5). Rage that has been caused by early humiliations – and that is suppressed and eventually repressed because one fears punishment and the withdrawal of love – can break through in adulthood. A person with this pattern may feel justified for indulging in an outbreak of rage or may wish to seek revenge for past disgraces in the hope of restoring his dignity and narcissistic equilibrium. But if it contradicts his ego ideal to play the part of the angry avenger, moral shame sets in. I feel it is extremely important for such archaic rage to be expressed within the therapeutic situation and for the analyst to accept it. Every attempt should be made to prevent such rage from remaining split off from consciousness and doing its unholy business autonomously – whether in a masochistic or sadistic fashion.

These remarks on narcissistic rage bring me to the close of this chapter, which has dealt with variations on the experience of shame and some hypotheses concerning their genesis and unconscious dynamics. In my final two chapters, I will take up questions concerning the analysis and treatment of neurotic susceptibility to shame.

6

MOTIFS OF SHAME
IN THE THERAPEUTIC
RELATIONSHIP

SHAME AS A REACTION TO
THE ANALYTIC SETTING

In my experience, the psychotherapeutic setting itself can cause certain reactions of shame. Thus I feel it is important to give some attention to this matter. Since most people who come to my practice are undergoing serious psychic difficulties, it is practically impossible for them not to be very anxious during the first meeting. There are those among the seekers of help who seem to be quite self-sufficient. They have no problem claiming their space or my attention, taking the initiative and setting the stage in the best possible way for themselves. But if one looks beneath the surface in such cases, one usually finds a scared performer who is "overdressed" – that is, overcompensating for his anxiety and embar-rassment by coming on strong. Most people seeking help show obvious signs of nervousness: sweaty hands, pale faces, uncertain eye contact, inhibited body movements, a tense or uneven tone of voice. Of course I do everything I can to put them at ease. And I would hardly succeed if I immediately jumped in and attempted to ferret out the sources of their fear and shame. The first session is not the right time for such probing. Clients want to tell me first of all what moved them to seek me out. If their level of anxiety climbs so high that even speech becomes laborious, I try to take the sting out by saying something like, "It must be an odd feeling to go to a complete stranger and to tell him personal things without hardly having said more than hello." Many people seeing me for the first time are very thankful for such a comment, assuming that it is based on authentic – as opposed to routine – empathy. It often has a relaxing effect on them because it lets them know that anxiety and inhibition are understandable in such a situation; they are to be regarded as natural reactions.

I myself do not feel entirely comfortable allowing such words as "anxiety," "inhibition" or even "shame" to enter the psychotherapeutic field too soon. It is as if a certain taboo were attached to those words – or at least a warning to use them with care and tact. While I feel it is fine during the first meeting to mention the possibility of feeling strange, weird, or lacking in complete trust, words such as anxiety or shame are more difficult to digest. For even in our psychologically enlightened, even somehow deformed, time, it is not always easy for clients – especially male ones – to admit their fears. It might be degrading to do so, since our fears do not fit in with our popular images of manhood. It is bad enough not to be able to get it together on one's own – having to call on the services of a psychotherapist. This is also the reason why no one should know anything about a client's visits, if possible. One counts on the therapist's professional discretion and hopes to avoid being seen by any other clients. In other words, just seeking out a psychotherapist can be a matter of shame.

Such a visit may even be kept a secret from one's companions, family, or friends. There are many respectable reasons for keeping a visit to a therapist a secret from one's spouse at the beginning. A woman may argue that her partner does not comprehend matters of the heart, or that he would get angry and perhaps jealous if he knew that she had emotional difficulties that she did not discuss with him. With men there may be the humiliation of not being thought of as man enough to stand on his own two feet. A man who visits a therapist may feel like a weakling and fear that he will be taken less seriously by his friends, colleagues, and especially his partner.

It was, however, the intention of the pioneers of psychoanalysis to create a setting that was as free as possible from anxiety and shame. In this spirit, Freud required analysands to say everything that came into their minds and analysts to abstain from any sort of criticism and judgment. Their sole job, he said, was to interpret the psychological connections neutrally. In Jungian practice, where Freud's basic rule was modified, and the psychoanalytic couch replaced with a face-to-face setting, the focus is on understanding the conscious and unconscious situation; an attempt is made to offer the analysand a protected space in which feelings of anxiety and shame become completely unnecessary. This does not, however, prevent their – sometimes forceful – re-emergence. But when they do emerge, one attributes them to transference and its resistances – repetitions of conflicts and patterns laid down in childhood. Returning to the here-and-now of the analytical situation, they can be worked on in the therapeutic dialogue. This momentous insight forms the basis of much of analytic psychotherapy since Freud.

But is the therapeutic setting truly conceived in such a way that all feelings of anxiety and shame can be nothing but repetitions of earlier experiences? I am skeptical. For the therapeutic situation really is "weird" – a person seeking help is supposed to trust a complete stranger with his or her most intimate – and perhaps embarrassing – concerns. Apart from the fact that the stranger may call himself a specialist in matters of the psyche, the client has no real connection with this person. Should it come as a complete surprise then, if the therapist's question "What brings you here?" fails to elicit an immediate and exhaustive outpouring of the heart?

Experience shows that there are many advantages to the guideline that a therapist should be a stranger and an outsider to the client's social circle. But this very unfamiliarity may make it all the more urgent for clients to question whether or not they can trust in this person. It is only natural that a client should feel anxious about the prospect of feeling small and ashamed, vulnerable and exposed as soon as he opens up. Is he not granting the therapist the power to hurt, reject, criticize, and belittle him – even to take advantage of his weakness?

We may well wonder whether such fears are caused by the therapeutic setting itself – the real situation – or if they have more to do with an expectation of being ashamed whose roots reach back into childhood. In other words, should these fears be attributed to the client's transference-fantasies? Considering the great variety of responses that individual clients have to the first therapeutic encounter, there can be no clear answer. Some potential analysands may feel so well understood by the therapist's way of listening and responding that they already experience relief from the weight of their shame-anxiety during the first hour – thus inspiring in them trust and hope for good things to come in the common therapeutic endeavor about to unfold. But in other cases, the client may feel so humiliated by the therapist's coldness and lack of empathy that he never returns, or at least resolves to stay on his guard against any further injury to his self-esteem. He may also conclude that the therapist has good reason not to take his whining so seriously. The therapist is after all the professional who knows what is best. Thus, we see how difficult it is to distinguish between a real assessment of the situation and a reaction based on transference. In fact, it would seem that there are hardly any real situations of any significance that do not unconsciously call up previously established ways of experiencing and reacting.

If he or she were connected only to the reality of the situation, a potential analysand might have a train of thought that could be expressed as follows: "My therapist is someone I don't know. He is more or less recognized as an authority in his field. I am coming to him for therapy, and I pay a fee. I remain free at all times to terminate the treatment; the therapist can not force me to continue. I have a right to be critically alert, to evaluate whether or not he has earned my trust. I intend to have my own say and do not need to surrender to his power of omniscience." But the very same reality might inspire another train of thought altogether, i.e. "I need psychotherapy because I am having an emotional crisis and I am confused. So how can I be sure that my therapist is not right when he interprets my doubts about his competence and my shame at his tactlessness as evidence of my resistance? Maybe I do need to work through this for the sake of my psychological growth." The reality is thus that although clients seem to have equal rights, and to be perfectly free to enter or exit a psychotherapeutic contract, therapists, in fact, are one up on their clients. They have command over a greater number of interpretations, which they may use to their own advantage. The patient is nearly always in a weaker position. (This does not mean that at certain points in the process the client may not make the therapist feel utterly useless, devalued, or blackmailed – for example by means of suicide-threats.) In any case, it is extremely difficult for people suffering from psychic wounds to sort out confidently whether they have come to the right place when they are deciding on a therapist, to know how seriously to take their doubts. Tilman Moser's detailed thoughts on this issue (1984) deserve close attention.

At the outset, the person who seeks help looks up to the therapist, feeling himself to be in an inferior or weaker position. As awkward and embarrassing as this may be for the client, it would be even harder to take if he had to see the therapist in the weaker role. Then how could he be expected to trust him? This is why most potential analysands look for an analyst who is substantially older and more experienced than they are. And it stands to reason. When we are physically ill, we are forced to place ourselves in the hands of the physician and to trust his competence. If we undergo surgery, we quite literally assume an inferior position – under the knife. But in these cases, we are only exposing our bodies. With the psychotherapist, we reveal our most secret thoughts and actions, dreams, fantasies, and feelings of shame and guilt. And we are not simply objects for the physician to act upon, but active partners; analytic psychotherapy can go nowhere without a degree of cooperation between analysand and analyst. Such cooperation requires a fundamental level of trust, and yet client and therapist seem not to be on the same level. In fact, most clients would rather look up to their therapists than regard them as peers – even though they often complain about it.

So what, then, is the meaning of the oft-repeated phrase "therapeutic partnership"? It was Jung's view that in deeper analyses "the doctor must emerge from his anonymity and give an account of himself, just as he expects his patient to do" (Jung 1935a: 23). Repeatedly we hear that the therapist, too, undergoes an analysis, that one half of every thorough-going analysis consists in the analyst's own self-examination. "By no device can the treatment be anything but the product of mutual influence, in which the whole being of the doctor as well as that of his patient plays its part" (Jung 1929: 163). But what does this mean in daily practice? Can such a motto be realized? I believe that the idea of a therapeutic partnership is crucial, but I also think that it should be relativized to some extent. Above all, we should not forget that this partnership falls within the boundaries set by a contract with specific goals. It never ceases to be an analysis or psychotherapy of the patient's emotional state. This means that the client's situation is not interchangeable with that of the therapist.

Clients should be able to use therapy and the therapist in the service of their developmental processes, as Winnicott said. They should feel as free as possible to report their troubles, conflicts, needs, their love for the analyst, as well as their hate and disappointment. Clients are granted the right to regress and may behave as childishly as they need to within the therapeutic setting. This is not always so easy, as fear of shame often keeps clients from letting go with the analyst.

Psychotherapists must under no circumstances let themselves go, even if their whole being seems to cry out for it. They must always put the patient's needs first, bringing the greatest alertness and sense of responsibility to all of their actions. They can not react thoughtlessly, return blows, requite love, punish, or retaliate. Long ago, Freudian psychoanalysts worked out a treatment technique with the aim of keeping a check not only on the patient's acting out, but also on the analyst's inappropriate emotional reactions. In Jungian analysis, where mutual influence is recognized as an important psychotherapeutic factor, no such technical rules are set. There is nothing to protect the analyst against the loss of therapeutic boundaries, emotional entanglements entered into in the name of spontaneity, mutual openness, and honest dialogue. Thus, all the more emphasis is put on a sense of personal responsibility for the client's inner world. In any case, the partnership of therapy is not based on equal footing.

As it happens, clients often complain about the lack of mutuality in the therapeutic relationship. They are quite justified in pointing out that although they know nothing of the therapist's private life, they are nonetheless supposed to tell him everything without withholding. It is impossible to deny this imbalance, and since knowledge does amount to power, it is no wonder that many clients feel as if they are at the mercy of one who knows so much about them. As the treatment continues, many clients understandably find it humiliating when the analyst becomes such an important part of their life and they feel, rightly or wrongly, like just one of many, valued only for professional reasons.

However we look at it, we cannot separate such feelings from the unavoidable and admittedly unnatural realities of the psychotherapeutic situation. Though individuals may have different reactions, therapeutic relationships are not the same as the natural relationships of real life. Relationships of love or friendship that provide satisfaction over a longer period of time are based on a balance of give and take, and of opening up to one another and setting boundaries. In comparison, the artificial inequality of the analytical situation may seem somewhat demeaning. It is not by accident that we speak of "undergoing" an analysis.

But is it really necessary to feel demeaned in this way? Is not the goal of analytical psychotherapy to strengthen one's sense of self-worth, rather than feelings of shame and degradation – as the very setting of therapy seems to do? Of course, one could object that an analysand who is embarrassed in front of his analyst suffers from a false shame that prevents him from accepting the "human, all-too-human" parts of himself. And yet it cannot be denied that there is something degrading about the analytical setting, a fact that clients sometimes use to justify their resistance: "I would feel much freer if our relationship were more natural. What can really come of it? Why should I expose the contents of my heart to you? At some point our relationship is going to end anyway." Or: "You always want to know everything about me. But I don't know the first thing about you. I don't know what you are really thinking." Or: "What does it means that you care for me? In the end you have to see the positive in everything; it's your job."

How can the analyst respond in such a situation without adding to the analysand's burden of shame? C.G. Jung often recommended that, as much as possible, analysts meet their patients "at the same level – not too high and not too low" (Jung 1935a: CW 18:337). He proposed that this would minimize the difficulties caused by transference (and, I might add, those caused by resistance). We have seen, however, that the analyst and analysand cannot meet in complete equality in the psychotherapeutic setting. Still, we should recognize that Jung's ideas represent a departure from classical Freudian technique. One of his most decisive modifications involves analytical anonymity, the idea that analysts should not show any human reactions and, in accordance with the rule of abstinence, should confine their remarks to the interpretation of unconscious conflicts. By contrast, Jung wanted to treat his analysands in a more "human" fashion, spontaneously entering into dialogue with them. Thus he introduced a very unorthodox style into the therapeutic encounter that has been like a liberating breeze for the analyst, bringing a freedom that I for one would not like to renounce.

Yet some analysts have misunderstood Jung's motto that the analyst should "give account of himself, just as he expects his patient to do" (Jung 1935a: 23) taking it as permission or even a directive to tell their dreams or describe how they deal with their own problems. Could this type of behavior help establish a better balance so that the patient does not feel so degraded by his or her unavoidably inferior position in the therapy? I, for one, have my doubts. For example, the analyst should beware of the danger that, with the best therapeutic intentions and in obedience to the mandate to give account of himself, he may unconsciously use the client for his own needs to get something off his chest. He may not realize what a burden this puts on the analysand, whose concerns he can easily lose sight of. In my opinion, analysts very rarely help their clients when they bring their own personal difficulties into the analysis in an attempt to have an encounter on the same level.

An example may illustrate what I mean. An analysand suffered from periodic mood swings that he described as deep holes. Often, it took only the slightest mishap to pull the rug out from under him such that he fell into an abyss of utter worthlessness. He would then feel completely devalued, ashamed even to show his face at work, where he had great responsibilities. It was clear that his feelings of degradation had little to do with reality. Instead, it was his merciless unconscious grandiosity that made such exaggerated demands on him, beating him down with feelings of total inadequacy. Therapeutically, I felt it was important not to leave him alone in these holes. He needed someone to empathically understand his suffering, though in the long run he would have to work through his problems in connection with the vicissitudes of a difficult life-history. In those critical moments, I tried to convey to him how he was losing all access to his positive human and professional qualities by falling into the trap of his inferiority complex. He usually felt better after such sessions, and it was not long before he was able to see the world and himself more realistically. However, in retrospect he would feel ashamed to have been such a cry-baby, dependent on my help for getting back on an even keel.

One day when he had fallen into one of his holes, I followed a spontaneous impulse by suggesting that I knew very well how this felt, having experienced something like it myself. It was only a brief hint, and – and this is very important – a true one, though perhaps more true to my past than my present. I offered it in a moment when I believed I could indeed comprehend how it must feel to be in his dungeon, on a spontaneous impulse to mitigate his shame and bring us more to the same level. But in the next session, he told me that my remark had made him feel misunderstood. When I said that I knew of such depressed states from personal experience, I only proved how incapable I was of imagining the extent of his suffering. To him, it was simply inconceivable that I could ever fall into such a hell. Apparently, my analysand still needed to idealize me, and thus it was impossible for me to do my part in bringing us to the same level.

Clearly it is not the analyst's personal confessions that bring mutuality to the therapeutic setting. It seems to me that the same level is more a product of the analyst's attitude, and especially his or her capacity for empathy; it depends on his or her willingness to seek out the level on which a meeting can take place with each individual client. Mutuality also comes about when analysts try to discover what part they play in any difficulties that may arise in the transference situation instead of always attributing all the problems to the client's pathology.

As far as addressing the one-sidedness of the therapeutic relationship, it seems to me most profitable for therapists to admit to their clients that their complaints are understandable and realistic. Therapists need to express their empathy for the suffering the necessary imbalance in the analytical situation causes their clients. The therapist's tone of voice will usually determine whether this will be perceived as condescending or not. Naturally, the client's suffering may also be connected to specific transference feelings, and can be used by him as a way of resisting. In such cases I have had good results by speaking directly to the matter, for instance, saying, "Something in you is so infuriated by the inequality of this relationship that it seeks to prevent us from working together. It would be a pity for you and for me if our therapy should fail because of this."

In short, I feel it is most important to affirm the analysand's sense that the analytic situation may be difficult to bear with and to do so before interpreting all difficulties as stemming from the transference or from resistance.

SEXUALITY

The cliché is still alive and well that analysis deals mainly with sexual issues. Thus analysands often expect – or fear – that the analyst will want to know all the details of his or her intimate life. Freud's perspectives have hardened into dogma. This is one reason why today many people specifically seek out an analyst of the Jungian persuasion. They have read or heard that Jungians do not regard everything as a sexual matter, and in fact take the spiritual dimension very seriously. What of this is true?

Jungian psychology also seeks the symbolic qualities of sexuality, in dreams, fantasies, and even in behavior. According to the "interpretation on the subjective level," for instance, sexual intercourse in dreams can be seen as a union of the ego with another part of the psyche, a *coniunctio* in the language of alchemy. This idea of a subjective level of interpretation is quite valuable. It turns our attention to the inner tendencies of the personality and helps bring them to consciousness. But we must also guard against the dangerous trap of playing down or glossing over the real physical acts that sexual drivenness can lead to. Feelings of shame about one's sexuality may affect both client and analyst, leading them to use symbolic interpretations as a way of avoiding painful and awkward issues. In such cases, interest in the subjective and symbolic level of interpretation becomes a defense, whether conscious or unconscious. This was not at all Jung's intention; I personally recall him saying as much. Still, misuse may be prevalent, if unintended, and we should be aware of the dangers.

It cannot be denied that sexuality can have its delicate aspects within analytic psychotherapy as well. How does the issue enter the dialogue? Of course every psychotherapist will have his or her way of approaching this and other issues. Personally, I prefer to allow analysands as much freedom as possible to discuss whatever they wish on their own terms, despite the fact that this very freedom can cause shame-anxiety. The client may worry that his or her particular concern will meet with rejection, that he will say something uncalled for or not right. Such fears of shame may reflect patterns of interaction laid down in childhood. As these patterns emerge in the transference, one has the therapeutic opportunity to elucidate them. But throughout the process I find it important to let the analysand be the one who raises the issues. Themes arising in dreams may be worthy of special consideration, however.

It can happen that an issue as important as sexuality simply does not come up for a long time. When this happens, I usually bring attention to the fact by saying something like, "Have you noticed that the issue of sexuality has never come up in our conversations, and seems to be bracketed out of your dreams as well?" This is an inviting gesture that shy people in particular are often grateful for. It can provide an occasion to reflect on why such an important issue has been neglected. Some analysands require such prodding before they can confess to having withheld all dreams containing sexual content. It may happen that the analysand simply did not report such dreams, especially if he or she suspected that they revealed embarrassing erotic feelings in the transference relationship toward the therapist. Often, such clients are relieved to be able to speak openly about such fantasies. But at other times, shame-anxiety and embarrassment about sexuality in general totally dominates the atmosphere. In these cases, in which the client has relegated sexuality to a taboo zone guarded by shame, it is important to trace the intrapsychic connections at the foundation of the taboo. Of course, it can happen that a person does not raise the issue of sexuality because he or she is enjoying a satisfying relationship and does not experience it as a problem, although this would be rare among people who seek therapy. Thus, if the client has overlooked the issue of sexuality, one must always question the motivation for the omission.

As I mentioned in the section on nakedness, the act of exposing one's body is archetypally associated with shame. Sexual intimacies tolerate no spectators. Seeing, as well as being seen, triggers the alarm of shame. This is not to say that we have no freedom when it comes to archetypal givens or that social attitudes and moral education do not influence an individual's tendency toward prudery or shameless desire to show off. Indeed, exhibitionistic and voyeuristic activities are attractive precisely because they disregard shame's warnings and seduce us with the "charm of the forbidden."

Even in pre-literate societies, where nearly all living space is shared, it is thought to be disturbing and highly improper to observe two persons engaged in intimate relations. In view of this, it is easier to understand the response of the client who once told me, "I find it difficult to speak with you, an outsider, about the details of my sexual life. That is something I can only do with my lover." Thus we might ask, are we justified in every case in interpreting such inhibitions as nothing more than neurotic defenses? Might there not be some archetypal root to barriers of shame that keep an observer from being privy to what should take place behind closed doors? And might not the same apply to the observer who happens to be an analyst? I would like to warn against judging as neurotic every feeling of shame that is bound up with the exposing of sexual activities and fantasies and advocate caution lest we confuse disrespectful unabashedness with a healthy attitude toward sexuality. Of course, by this I do not mean to shy away from an analyst's responsibility to help a client win greater flexibility and freedom in dealing with his or her sexuality and its attendant shame-anxiety. I am only making a plea for analytical tact, and for the empathy that is often necessary to avoid making the barriers of shame yet more rigid. The same advice applies to all issues invested with shame, which contribute so powerfully to resistance against analysis.

In my experience, there are certain sexual issues that are especially likely to be imbued with shame. One such issue enters the therapeutic field when an analysand feels it necessary to confess that – although he is involved in a relationship – he still masturbates. The client often experiences this as a defeat, and consequently feels a degrading loss of self-respect. The intensity of his feelings of shame may have no relation to the frequency with which he masturbates – whether he indulges in the vice several times daily or only once in a while.

A 35-year-old man occasionally felt overwhelmed by the compulsion to buy pornographic magazines that stimulated his masturbatory activities. Afterward he felt so soiled that he became depressed for days and had serious difficulty concentrating. It was many months before he could overcome his shame and begin talking about it in analysis. When he reported that he dreamed repeatedly of a dog that pestered, barked, and sniffed at him, I suggested the interpretation that perhaps he could not keep from feeling like a dirty dog. In dreams, dogs, with their noses for things can symbolize instinctive intuition. Thus I told him that it seemed he was afraid someone nearby, perhaps his analyst, might sniff him out and see through him in some way. For the first time he was able to talk about how ashamed he was of his habit of taking pornographic magazines with him to bed to masturbate.

This is not the place to explore the complex problem of the compulsion to masturbate – which may stem from many different kinds of unconscious motivation. In this context we are interested above all in the meaning of shame. Shame in connection with masturbation is sometimes mixed with feelings of guilt. For example, a married man once told me that he felt guilty toward his wife, since he was robbing her of something that belonged to her.

But what is the meaning of the extraordinarily intense feelings of shame so often associated with masturbation? Is it a shame based merely on upbringing and collective norms, a fear of not being normal in sexual matters? Or might it amount to a kind of *Leidensdruck* – a meaningful suffering that motivates one to search out the deeper problem, of which masturbation is just a symptom. In the first case, shame about masturbation would be society's way of punishing individuals who succumb to unacceptable sexual practices – dealing a blow to their self-esteem. But the question remains as to what prevents the affected person from accepting his practice, which, after all, is a purely private matter? In forbidding it, is he not setting himself up for defeat, preparing himself for repeated tortures of self-loathing? In practice, it is sometimes possible to reduce the intensity of the compulsive drive by helping the client ease up on his self-punishment. Once again, a compulsion to masturbate that triggers a violent sense of shame is usually symptomatic of deeper disturbances, which should gradually make their way into the spotlight of analysis. In such cases it is seldom productive to remain at the level of the symptom. Yet if the tension has been relaxed to the extent that masturbation can be experienced and accepted as a form of autonomous pleasure and release (*Selbstbefriedigung*) an important step will have been reached. Of course, in this one must not deny the painful awareness that masturbation is a substitute pleasure implying much loneliness.

As a well-known rule-of-thumb, in analytic psychotherapy one avoids dealing directly with symptoms, since these are merely expressions of more profound disturbances. This naturally also applies to those sexual problems that cause a person to seek out a therapist – usually frigidity among women, and complications of potency among men. That impotence and frigidity usually indicate more general relationship problems has become a truism today. Yet one must also be aware that quite often deeper personality disturbances are at the heart of such relationship difficulties. For those who seek a therapist for help with sexual difficulties, the whole subject of sex is likely to have been relegated to a dark and shameful realm of taboo. Therapists who work with these people meet with a strong "shame-resistance" as soon as the issue of sexual acts and experiences comes up. Therefore it seems important in such cases to deal therapeutically with resistance based on shame and to move with care toward an investigation of its background. Sometimes it is only by means of a "resistance analysis" – possibly a prolonged one – that one can get access to the emotions and fantasies connected with the problem. This is especially important when this shame not only causes resistance in the therapeutic relationship but also functions as a taboo in the love relationship. Thus it represents a momentous step forward when the atmosphere of trust in therapy has evolved to the point where the client can disclose the private details of his sex life, especially the disturbing moments. Quite apart from the cathartic effect that such sharing can have for the client, it allows therapists to empathize more precisely with the particular difficulties and conflicts that may be at the root of the disturbance. In spite of the rule of thumb that says dealing directly with the symptom is a technical error, such moments of empathic understanding can often be therapeutically helpful. On the other hand, direct advice to the client about how to modify or refine his or her sexual technique usually is not very effective, as generally the problem is not so much one of technique as of erotic fantasies suppressed by anxiety, inhibition, and shame. However, even direct advice can be of some benefit if, in giving it, the therapist conveys a liberated or natural attitude toward sexuality.

There is, however, one drawback that should be mentioned about discussions of sexuality. They may stimulate excess attention to the matter that may block a spontaneous surrender to sexual energy. Even a single thought about the possibility of failing sexually may be enough to throw the whole instinctive program of sexual functions out of kilter, as if an inner observer had taken up his obtrusive post. For example, an analysand who was inhibited sexually, and who often suffered from difficulties with potency with his wife, had the following dream: in the middle of intercourse, he noticed his father watching him with a telescope from a window of the house next door. In reality, his authoritarian know-it-all father had caused the analysand a great deal of pain. As a consequence, he had learned to always keep an eye on his own spontaneous impulses. It was as if he had introjected his father's critical eye. The father's strictness probably contained a degree of sadism, mobilized unconsciously to ward off his erotically tinged joy over his son's budding masculinity in adolescence. Thus it made sense that the subject of sex was taboo in the family. In the analytical situation it was clearly necessary – especially after the analysand presented the aforementioned dream – to ask whether he also experienced me, "the analyst-father," as a voyeur, someone who wanted to spy on his intimate life and disturb his sexual spontaneity.

Thus in therapy, it is important for the barriers of shame to become more flexible and for the realm of sexuality to become a freer subject of dialogue. But one must also keep in mind that an overdose of reflection on the topic of sexuality can inhibit one's instinctive spontaneity. However, the client's resistances with regard to sexuality can join secretly with those of the therapist. This effectively brackets out of the analytical encounter particular aspects of sexual experience that may be the very shame-bound details that are at the source of the disturbance that needs to be treated. To stress a therapeutic attitude of respecting resistances, dealing with symptoms indirectly, and avoiding an overdose of reflection about the topic are all ways of justifying this evasive behavior. It seems to me that the art of analysis requires finding a good middle way. If analysts are fated to be observers and to trigger the inner observing authority in the analysand, this function can at least be conducted in a way that is tolerant, emboldening, and encouraging of spontaneity.

The analyst, too, may experience a degree of more or less conscious shame-anxiety stemming from his fantasy of being seen by the patient as an indiscreet voyeur stimulated by the patient's stories about his sexual experiences. I do not believe that just because they assume the customary professional persona – taking a neutral, matter-of-fact attitude toward the patient's secrets – analysts should imagine that they are completely free of voyeuristic tendencies. It is more likely that they do occasionally experience fantasies of an erotic nature. After all, psychotherapists are human. This makes it all the more important for them to allow their fantasies to come to awareness, for only when fantasies are conscious can they be kept under control. In some circumstances, these may also represent aspects of a "syntonic" countertransference, in which case they function as an indicator of unconscious processes taking place in the patient – which can be of great help in the therapeutic process.

On rare occasions patients report their most intimate sexual experiences in a markedly shameless fashion. This calls to mind an experience that occurred in my practice. At one point, I realized that I was growing increasingly embarrassed as I listened to two different patients describe their most intimate experiences in graphic detail. It went against the grain for me to realize my discomfort, because until then I had seen myself as someone with a liberated attitude, free of any trace of prudishness. But in both these cases, the atmosphere in the therapeutic field became increasingly charged with sexual energy until it became clear to me that these stories were intended to seduce me – in one case rather deliberately, in the other perhaps less so. Now patients have the "right" to such impulses. It is best if, in the analysis, these can make their way into the client's consciousness and be accepted and understood by the therapist. As long as they remain unconscious, or at least unexpressed, they create a therapeutic atmosphere that is strangely tense and thick. Once the analysand admits to these wishes, however, the therapist may not under any circumstances act to fulfill them. Even if the initiative were to come from the patient, such a consummation would amount to a breach of the therapeutic relationship and an abuse of trust that can cause serious emotional harm (Jacoby 1984: 105–13; Wirtz 1989).

The countless nuances of love and sexuality that come to expression in the analytical encounter may trigger shame-anxieties in the analyst as readily as in the client. Not only does this fact need to be accepted, but also, if handled appropriately, it may have an important therapeutic function. For one thing, feeling empathy and respect for a client's shame boundaries contributes to a therapeutic sense of tactfulness. It sensitizes therapists to how close they can come to a particular patient's secrets. An analyst's own shame-anxiety may help him or her to better sense of a particular individual's unique threshold of shame. This is in no way meant to contradict the general therapeutic goal of freeing analysands from the tyranny of shame. Ultimately, the quest is for what Aristotle calls the "pure truth" (as opposed to "general opinion"). On the way to this goal, it is often possible to dissolve identifications with "general opinion" and so overcome acquired shame. We will return to this theme later.

On the other hand, it would seem that in the present social climate, sexual taboos have lost much of their power. There has been a definite increase in public tolerance of extra-marital sexuality and even homo-sexual relations – at least on the surface. The spread of AIDS may have curbed promiscuity somewhat, but an active sex life is still a value worthy of aspiration. Consequently, persons who for some reason cannot keep up with this trend tend to feel ashamed. Because of their unlived (sex)lives, they may feel incomplete as men or women and suffer a general sense of being exluded and devalued. They may expect their analysts to devalue them as well – another reason why the subject of sexuality may be fraught with shame and only approachable for discussion after a great deal of inhibition has been overcome. This brings us to a subject to be covered in the next chapter, concerning shame and feelings of devaluation that go beyond the issue of sexuality.

SINGLENESS AND LONELINESS

I don't know of many people who find it easy to spend their lives without a partner, even if today's society offers many possibilities for dealing creatively with singleness and constructing a satisfying life without marriage. Being single is still a problem for women especially, although I know a good number of men who also are troubled about not being able to find the right partner, even if they are not exactly starved for sex.

The pathos of singleness is two-fold. Not only is there an unsatisfied longing for love, for emotional and physical togetherness, but there may also be the shame that comes from being regarded by the world as unloved and undesirable.

Even in this age of feminism and greater recognition of professional and single women, the old values still retain their power, consciously or unconsciously. Thus the woman without a husband – or even a partner – is often found worthy of pity.

It is extremely demeaning to feel that one is being pitied. One feels devalued and belittled – sensations that can trigger mistrust even toward persons who really care. One begins to suspect everyone of being just another person who comes to pity one – and secretly gloat. This is especially true when these others are married or have partners. They trigger a feeling of being secretly despised and disparaged.

At the same time, single persons are often intensely jealous of those who have taken the plunge of getting involved in partnership, marriage, or family. Sometimes they even feel poisoned by their feelings of envy. As a

90

defense, there arises an impulse to demean or deprecate those that one envies, calling them conservative and boring, or dismissing them for their narrow-mindedness. Those who catch themselves in this maneuver often react with shame to their own impulses, putting themselves down to an even greater extent.

For centuries, unmarried women have been regarded as of little social value – a prejudice which has put them at a grave disadvantage. Even today, the custom of making fun of frustrated spinsters persists. In spite of considerable progress in the struggle for equality and autonomy for women, a patriarchal specter continues to exert its power – only valuing a woman if she has a man at her side. As much as anywhere, this specter is powerfully at work in the psyches of women themselves. In a single woman, it may make her feel incomplete, and assume that everyone thinks she could not find a man, was passed over and scorned. Thus she suffers from the disgrace of the unloved. Single men also suffer from loneliness, but they are not usually prone to this sort of shame reaction. Even if he stays a bachelor, a man is not subject to such intense discrimination. At most, he must fend off rumors that he is homosexual, which he may perceive as discrimination.

The task of analysis is to call such collective norms into question and thereby reduce their power – especially when they stand in the way of individuation. But norms are often unbelievably stubborn, especially when they are embedded in the disturbed interrelational patterns resulting from early childhood wounds. In such cases it is not only social norms that have a devaluing effect. The root of the problem lies in self-rejection, even self-hatred, which is experienced in projected form as disapproval by others.

The shame-anxiety of having to face the world as a pitiful wallflower is not unrelated to the psychic wounding that, in many cases, is responsible for one's unchosen state of singleness. The matter needs to be viewed within the broadest possible context. It is clear that unwanted singleness can have a variety of causes, one of which is surely lack of trust, both in someone else and in oneself. Without trust there is no possibility of opening oneself to a relationship.

It is generally known that a person's ability to trust and distrust others appropriately stems from his childhood history. Too many children, having been traumatically shamed, construct a thick, protective wall of mistrust around themselves. Throughout their lives, they avoid at all costs the repetition of those horrible feelings of pain and humiliation they endured as children. Consequently, anyone who treads too near awakens intense distrust and fears of being used and degraded all over again. As soon as one is open – and thus vulnerable – misgivings arise. Worst of all, one may not have learned to differentiate between those who can be trusted and those who cannot. Thus a vicious circle is set in motion: an impenetrable barrier of shame prevents anyone from coming close enough to discover how weak and needy I am. I want to be sure that no one is given the power to reject, hurt, and put me to shame again. So I seek protection behind a mask that conveys the message, "I am unapproachable." But if this warning signal works, no one will even attempt to come near me. Thus, once again, I find myself alone, convinced that no one loves me.

One way to defend against this terrible sense of rejection is to give the impression that I am perfectly complete without friends or intimate relationships. But I cannot let others see how much I suffer from loneliness, so I must keep them at a distance. I may die of hunger and thirst, from a lack of interpersonal relationships, but I am ashamed to admit this even to myself, and definitely hope to keep it a secret from others. The closeness that I long for in the final analysis can only mean opening myself to potential disgrace and humiliation. It seems too dangerous to risk a new experience that would reassure me that my fears are unfounded, that I need not transfer a childhood pattern onto every possible partner or let a wall of fear and shame come between me and every new experience.

The inner world of someone who suffers in this fashion is ruled by a cruel dictator, a figure who can often be seen in dreams. Motifs of persecution and imprisonment are common in such dreams. For example, a person dreams of awaiting execution in a concentration camp. Of course other motifs also occur as well: being alone in the desert or sinking in desert sands, for example. It is as if those who suffer from this self-rejection carry within themselves a pattern of interaction accompanied by a tape that says, "Whatever I do, feel, say, or wish always meets with rejection. I can't ever do the right thing for anyone. I can never win their loving approval." In very serious cases, one would have to speak of a primary shame in which the pattern of interaction communicates the inner message that "I should hide my face from the world. I am not fit to be human for I am unworthy of love." This represents the most basic experience of rejection, which offers no alternative but to feel devalued and despised. Expectations, longings, and needs for love and care are only there to be suppressed. One treats oneself the way one's parental figures seem to have treated one as an infant. Whatever the parents actually did or did not do, the child grew up with a destructive inner pattern of interaction.

One yields to the most hated parental figure in spite of the hurt and degradation they have caused, because they depict strength and success, which the child idealizes. The child idealized this apparent strength. Identification with such a parental figure establishes a pattern of inter-action in the growing person that communicates the inner message, "If I want to amount to anything, I have to be strong and conquer my need for care. I have to admit to as few feelings as possible." This kind of pseudo-pride seems necessary if I am to retain some vestige of self-esteem. But as soon as this pride is the least bit shaken, unbearable feelings of shame threaten to invade.

I have attempted here to describe an intra-psychic pattern that may lie beneath the shame-anxiety associated with being lonely and single. The analyst must meet this dynamic with empathy. There is a feeling of being unloved or unworthy that pervades one's entire being, and which may, in a number of ways, be suffered through, fended off, or compensated for. It should be added that men also suffer from the wound of rejection that I have described, berating themselves for being unable to enter into any substantial partnership. But their singleness is less complicated than a woman's because it does not carry the additional burden of social discrimination.

Whatever the deeper causes of their singleness, the task for many women must be to make a satisfying life for themselves without an intimate partner. This becomes an especially pressing concern by the time they have reached their more mature years. Then the goal of strengthening their self-confidence has first priority. With or without therapeutic help, this task begins with a process of seeing through and thus disarming the inner, often unconscious patriarchal specter that devalues single women by regarding them as incomplete. This work creates a foundation for improved self-confidence and thus leads to greater freedom in living one's own life.

And yet one should never underestimate the profound suffering that being single often causes. This kind of suffering cannot be compared with the hurt partners inflict on each other. Even when they make life a living hell for each other, or their children plague them with endless worries, the suffering of married people is qualitatively different from that of someone who is alone. What is most painful in the plight of the single person is the sense of not belonging, of being excluded from an essential part of life.

Analysts who are married do not come by easy answers for these clients, if they do not want to sound trite or pat. In my experience it sometimes feels as if I practically had to be ashamed for being so much luckier in this respect – a question I usually attribute to the phenomenon of "syntonic countertransference" (Fordham 1957). In other words, by means of my own reaction of shame, I perceive the patient's fear of feeling shamed by me, the fear that I would look upon her condescendingly. For example, an analysand fears that, deep down, I find her as unworthy of love as everyone else does. In any case, she cannot believe I would be able to comprehend the quality and extent of her suffering. If she happens to sense that I can indeed empathize with her situation, this may trigger a fear of closeness. To protect herself from the possibility of being understood, she might attribute to me motives of pity and condescension. After all, in her eyes, my position can only be compared to that of the enviable rich, who reduce others to the status of pitiful beggars by giving them alms.

Such are the fantasies that often dominate the therapeutic field – which the analysand has to endure no less than the analyst. Many of these same patients are ashamed to realize that they sometimes feel envy toward me and my life, which seems – in whatever imagined respect – so much better. It often takes years before the bond of trust between us becomes durable enough, for in their experience the analyst is often a cruel, raping intruder capable of causing unspeakable shame. Therapeutically, it may be of decisive importance for the analyst to survive the entire onslaught of rejection, suspicion, and resistance, in order to prove his ability to be there as a therapeutic ally.

With that, we come to our final chapter, and a discussion of analytic-psychotherapeutic approaches to strengthening trust in oneself and finding liberation from constrictive shame-anxiety and susceptibility to shame.

7

PSYCHOTHERAPY WITH PROBLEMS OF SELF-ESTEEM AND SUSCEPTIBILITY TO SHAME

INTERACTIONAL PATTERNS, THE SHAME COMPLEX, AND THE TRANSFERENCE

As we discussed in an earlier chapter, feelings of self-esteem are founded on the empathic care and affirmation one received from significant others early in life. This has become a sort of psychological truism, especially since the publications of Spitz and Winnicott, as well as Neumann and others. Modern infant research confirms these links, if with different nuances. In particular, the writings of Daniel Stern present a detailed description of how various interactional patterns that have their origins in the relationship between infant and mother influence all later relationships and are particularly relevant to the relationship between patient and analyst. Early relationship patterns also play a decisive role with regard to problems of shame-anxiety and susceptibility, since shame is based primarily on the fear of losing value in the eyes of others, even if those others are only figures of fantasy. Self-esteem, like shame-anxiety, has an interpersonal origin, and yet it is precisely shame that sends us into isolation or retreat.

People who consult a psychotherapist place themselves in an interactive field similar in certain ways to the "primal relationship," in which the maternal caretaker carried out the function of self-regulating other. Frequently, clients hope that the psychotherapist can somehow relieve their psychic suffering, and rescue them from their depressive self-doubt. Unfortunately, the therapist cannot effectively assume this function, since the analysand is not an infant and the analyst is not its mother. Analytical psychotherapy requires the analysand's active collaboration. The outcome of analysis depends not only on his or her conscious efforts, but also on whether the Self – the organizational center of the personality as a whole – can be constellated in a cooperative way.

Yet in many ways, the basic forms of early mother–infant interaction, together with the relevant sense of self, remain active for a lifetime. The following example from my practice should illustrate this. A young

95

student consulted me complaining that he found it hard to sit in a lecture hall because he was tormented by the fantasy that everyone could hear him swallowing, which would make them notice and look at him. This prevented him from concentrating on the professor and his lecture. All he could think of were his embarrassing swallowing noises, which made him feel horribly awkward. He was clearly suffering from symptomatic shame-anxiety, feeling exposed, observed by the others. This then put his autonomy in jeopardy. He chose me as his analyst because he had read a book of mine that made him feel understood. And in the initial interview, according to his report, he found that he was comfortable with both my age and the atmosphere of my consulting room. During the first three or four meetings we worked mostly on his main difficulty, namely, the trouble he had in marking out the boundaries of his own domain. After I told him that psychotherapy should help him gain a greater sense of what it feels like to be himself, he suddenly felt much more self-confident. For the first time, he reported, he was able to tell himself, "I am who I am," and it really helped him to an astonishing degree. Above all, he ascribed this transformation to a sort of magical power that I, his analyst, apparently had at my disposal.[6] I, too, was amazed at the suddenness of this transformation, knowing full well that it would never last. Indeed, the recovery lasted a few months, but after a long vacation break and the suffering of a disappointment, my patient fell back into the familiar old shame-anxiety. He was no longer buoyed up by the magical power he had previously experienced in my presence. On the contrary, he now felt this as an influence working against him. As before, I continued to have too much influence. But now this very influence made him feel profoundly shaken and virtually incapable of remaining himself in my presence.

How are we to view this episode psychologically? In my experience as an analyst, such an immediate improvement is rather unusual. It is clear that initially, I performed the function of a good, protective, self-regulating mother. As far as I could see, his improvement had nothing to do with me or the few interpretations I had made, but rather with this function of the self-regulating other that the patient had unconsciously delegated to me. The magical powers that he ascribed to me can be explained with reference to an archetypal realm that underlies the mother of the primal relationship. It is expressed in the mythic conception of a "Great Mother" or mother goddess, which Erich Neumann has described so well (1955). It should be noted here, however, that the idea of an immensely powerful mother goddess is a symbolic formulation attributed retrospectively to early experiences that are preconscious, prior to the development of speech and representation.

All of this should help explain why the smallest evidence of a shadow falling on my perfection was enough to plunge my patient into deep disappointment. His alliance with my magical powers broke down, throwing him back onto himself. Suddenly he became conscious of his dependency on me – someone who had been abandoning him for weeks at a time while on vacation – and ashamed of it as well. Mistrust and shame-anxiety also took over – all of them expressions of interaction patterns acquired in early childhood, repeated now in the transference to me.

This example shows why the analyst can not simply assume the function of the other that regulates the self of the patient. First and foremost it should be said that, if he is to be therapeutically effective, the analyst must take his cues from the analysand's unconscious. Whatever the therapist does, whether interpreting, confronting, empathizing, or just reacting, the decisive factor is the manner in which the analysand receives, interprets, and understands it. For the analyst to really assume the function of a new and better self-regulating other, the analysand must give up his mistrustful defenses and overcome his shame of dependency, even if this shame might be justified to some extent. Regression to the stage of the infant is not always necessary, but deconstruction of a defensive and falsely autonomous shell is. The important thing is for the analyst to gain access to the feelings of the wounded child, as described in detail by Asper (1993) and Mattern-Ames (1987). It goes without saying that all of this takes place on a symbolic plane, since the analyst is not the mother. At best, the patient will experience the analyst as if he were a new self-regulating other. Though this transformative event takes place within the psyche of the analysand, the analyst is an instrumental and indispensable part of it.

But before any of this can occur, the analysand's unconscious interaction patterns must be activated in the analysis, drawing the analyst sooner or later into their drama. In Jungian terms, this means that the patient's perception of the analyst is distorted in accordance with whatever "complex" is activated. Kast correctly noted that "the complexes illustrate relationships and all the related emotions and stereotypical behavior patterns experienced in childhood and later life" (Kast 1992: 158). This history of relationships tends to make its way into the analysis as well. For example, in the case of the analysand described above, once his initial fusion with my omnipotence had dissolved, he returned to his old, all-too-familiar relationship pattern. If he were to put his fantasy and expectation into words, it might read: "They push me up against the wall. They do not hear anything I say, so what I have to say must be dumb. All I can do is retreat into my shell. Only then will I be noticed. Suddenly they will turn their attention to me, the sulking child. It is embarrassing to be exposed like this, to be made the center of attention, but at least then I will be noticed. My powerful, successful father, whose only concern is harmony in the family, tries everything to get me to stop sulking. He wants so badly to reassure himself of my love. But nothing works. I can not get out of my little pit, even though I feel so lonely here. I feel ashamed to stay in it, yet it would be even more humiliating to let myself be rescued."

This relationship pattern now came to encompass the therapeutic field between us. For a long time he arrived at his sessions full of fear, worrying about falling into a shameful situation. He was upset when he came and would tell me how nervous he felt, but after that he could hardly utter another word. It was horribly embarrassing to fall into such stubborn silences, but it was stronger than the two of us. At times he indicated he was beginning to assert himself more effectively in his outer life. I was convinced that this was true, but it still sounded as if he were mainly telling me this in order to appease me, and perhaps himself as well. He wanted me to understand that in spite of everything, our efforts were not completely in vain. For he also demanded a great deal of himself. Indeed, a rather merciless "grandiose self" drove him on, especially in his studies. He needed his teachers to acknowledge him as unusually smart and talented, and the smallest criticism could bring him crashing down. He never allowed himself to remain paralyzed for long, however, but worked day and night to eradicate any weaknesses. As sensitive as he was to criticism, he was also very embarrassed by praise, which caused him an overwhelming shame-desire.

Consequently, he was very determined to be a cooperative and worthy analysand, which made it all the more difficult when we both fell prey to his complex-ridden interaction patterns. Though I sensed his desperation when he was imprisoned in his shell, there was hardly anything either of us could do about it. For example, as soon as I attempted to speak to his desperation, I sensed that I was coming too close. Thus I felt like his father, who tried with all his might to gain his son's good favor in order to restore the peace. It was clear that in such moments he experienced me the same way. Sometimes when I asked him questions and communicated my interest to him, he was relieved, but usually these interventions felt too active and intrusive, forcing him to withdraw even further into his shell. But if I allowed him to stew in his own juices, he felt distressed with himself and abandoned by me. In time, he was able to bring this last feeling to expression, although in a highly indirect fashion. This was because his desire to receive care and attention from me (or his father or a significant other) was closely bound up with shame. Offering him interpretations was very awkward as well. At times he was able to communicate certain of his difficulties in sparse, telegrammatic style. Sometimes, if I tried to elaborate on them, putting them in a possible psychological context, he envied my knowing better and felt more than ever like he was standing in my shadow. Repeatedly he remarked that my influence on him was too strong, that it blocked him; he felt he was weak for attuning himself so much to me, that this made me too important in his life. The result of all this ambivalence was that he could neither remain true to himself nor adequately form a relationship with me. Whatever I did, I was powerless against the "influence" that he felt emanating from me, and blocking him completely. One of his dominant fantasies was that his issues were not heard by the other, and that it would be too embarrassing to express them. How often did he tell me that he had something to report, but something "that did not belong to the analysis." All the while, he was quite aware that everything that concerned him was important for the analysis.

Along with my empathy for his lousy situation, I also became aware of feeling anger, anger that grew as time went on. I was angered by my impotence in the face of his obstinate resistance, by his power to put me in a powerless position. It soon became apparent that this was an unconscious power game that belonged also to his interaction patterns. So I decided to confront him with this power game, show him what a destructive effect his need for such an illusory satisfaction was having on the analysis, and how he was only defeating himself by it. To an extent, the confrontation was successful, helping to break the vicious circle that we had been caught in. The breakthrough, in my opinion, took place on three levels. First, the analysand was made to confront our therapeutic goals and challenged to see how he was sabotaging the very improvement he was hoping for. Second, blunt confrontations, it appears, had not been one of his interaction patterns, not being common in his family. Thus this was to a certain extent a new experience for him, and together with the third factor, gave him a new start: I had spoken of the power game between us, how he had in a sense become more powerful than I and was able to exercise tyranny over me by virtue of his attitude of refusal. Now someone who is able to exercise such power no longer has to suffer from being shamefully small and powerless. Thus my analysand no longer felt wholly subservient to my "influence" and its shameful effect; he also had the power to castrate me, so to speak, a fatherly authority figure. Thus the accusation in my intervention simultaneously allowed him to have a higher estimation of his personality and potential effectiveness. At least he bore the harshness of the confrontation well – indeed, it was as though he had been waiting for it.

In the same session, I also asked him whether he could not see any other way than always letting my influence block him and thus give himself an excuse to escape into a passive victim role. Could he not perhaps make an active attempt to imagine what this "influence" was like? For example, he could make a picture or drawing of it in order to discover its contours. He agreed and, after this session he proceeded to draw various large, erect, male sex organs – phalli – which in his fantasy he associated with his father (or with me, as a fatherly transference figure). Then suddenly he decided to attach one of these penises to a drawing of himself. This symbolic gesture awakened within him a sense of the activity, initiative, and masculine energy that he had previously identified with his father and with my influence. Thus began a process that moved him toward greater freedom and initiative, while his shame-anxieties and inhibitions began to fade.

Soon thereafter, he fell deeply in love for the first time in his life. Suddenly, he became amazingly active and overcame many inhibitions. All of the hopes and disappointments that this experience brought up made him feel intensely alive. There was something else very crucial about this experience: it could be communicated to others and understood; it could be shared, as the joy and woe of love is an eternal human theme. Thus he felt for the first time that to be himself did not necessarily require slinking off into a god-forsaken pit; on the contrary, he could see himself as a fully normal man belonging to the human race.

I hope this example illustrates how various interaction patterns can shape the patient–analyst relationship, and how difficult it can be to loosen the grip of such patterns in order to allow for a development to continue that, at best, leads to an increase in self-confidence.

Generally speaking, we can say that psychic complexes with their corresponding interaction patterns are constantly being activated in the here and now – especially in the analytical situation, as elements of the transference. Hence it is crucial that the analyst make himself available as a figure of transference. This can only happen if he allows himself to participate emotionally with the client, sensitively reading his own reactions as indicators of the analysand's needs. Together with the patient, the analyst enters the therapeutic field characterized by the mutual influence of each psyche on the other. "Syntonic" counter-transference and empathy are indispensable instruments for navigating this psychic terrain. The former refers to the possibility that the analyst's own emotional reactions will provide him with "hunches" about the patient's unconscious processes (Fordham 1957). Considering that within the therapeutic field the analyst is influenced by the unconscious of the patient, he may develop antennae that enable him to perceive certain vibrations and even discreet elements of the patient's experience. These counter-transferential insights always require verification, however, since they could just as easily spring from the analyst's own unconscious processes, projected onto the patient (cf. Fordham 1957; Jacoby 1984).

In this context, I have elected to use the term "interaction pattern" rather than the Jungian term "complex." Of course, the idea of interaction is implied in the notion of a complex, even if it is not spelled out. In Jungian language, interaction patterns can be seen as contents of the personal unconscious in so far as generally human (archetypal) needs come to expression in the individual's life. In other words, generally human life-issues stem from archetypal roots that underlie the complexes in the personal unconscious. Experientially, interaction patterns and complexes are very closely related. In my view, a complex is the feeling tone or affective value that resides in a particular interaction pattern. Though the notion of interaction patterns (Stern's RIGs) might seem to emphasize only an objective, outer level of experience, we should not forget that, like complexes, these are composed primarily of images and fantasies. They come to expression as figures in dreams, for example, embodying our expectations about interactions with others. The characteristic ways that we relate to the figures of our dreams represent interaction patterns. Though appearing as figures of the outer world – parents, friends, superiors, enemies, strangers, etc. – they are at the same time figures of our fantasy, of our inner world.

Whenever possible, analysis should get to the bottom of the emotions involved in interaction patterns by delving into the memories, dreams, fantasies, anxieties and feelings of shame attached to them. Such is the repetition aspect of analysis that it provokes an emotional re-living of old conflicts and wounds. However, this differs from a simply literal repetition, in that it takes place in a therapeutic environment in which empathic understanding is brought to bear on old, still-virulent injuries. The patient is often taken by surprise by such understanding at first, fending it off with mistrust. Yet eventually, it becomes the basis for a newfound tolerance and understanding of his or her own way of being with all its weaknesses and conflicts.

As I have said, it may take some time for a patient to begin to trust such understanding, especially when old interaction patterns keep asserting themselves, distorting the lens with distrust.

Of course, the analyst brings his or her own complexes and their corresponding interaction patterns into the therapeutic situation. To the extent that they are unconscious, these can disturb and distort the analyst's understanding of the patient and impair the analytical process. Thus a thorough training analysis is absolutely imperative for all future analysts. At the least, analysis should sensitize the therapist to the possibility that he can, at any time, fall prey to his own illusory projections and counter-transference distortions. It should also help him develop a capacity to critically examine and modify his perspective, without losing his own identity or integrity in the process. In any case, the capacity for empathic understanding is of crucial significance for the practice of analysis. I find the expression understanding (*Verständnis*) particularly apt because it encompasses both psychological cognition (*Verstand*) and empathic recognition of a wide range of viewpoints. The patient, allowing himself to feel understood and to grow in his empathy for his own wounds and shortcomings, undermines his expectation, or fear, that those around him will respond to him according to his habitual interaction patterns. In other words, he will withdraw his projections to some extent, and will begin to see others with newer, clearer eyes. The dissolution of an entrenched interaction pattern may at first be unsettling, but it is necessary if change is to occur. As an example, I would like to return to the patient who slowly came to experience me as something other than just an influence undermining his independence. Slowly, albeit with some lapses, he developed the ability to remain himself in my presence and to initiate activities.

From a Jungian perspective, one might say that the natural developmental and organizational tendency of the Self, previously frustrated by negatively limiting interaction patterns, has been reactualized. In such cases, fixation gives way to movement and interactions gain more vitality. We might ask whether this occurs because inner figures and representations have changed with the effect of accommodating to the patient's new freedom and self-affirmation, or whether it is the sense of self that first experiences the growth spurt, only initiating secondarily a change of attitude on the part of the inner figures. This question is probably no more answerable than the famous question about the chicken and the egg. However, either way, a transformation of the psychic state is implied as well, and thus also new forms of interaction with significant others.

There is empirical evidence to show that in a deep analysis or psychotherapy, the figures of the inner world – intrapsychic representations – often do change. This can most clearly be seen in dreams. I have witnessed several dream series in which punishing fathers changed over time into supportive inner figures. At times, the impetus for the transformation came from the dream-ego. For example, persecuting men turned into friends as soon as the female dreamer no longer tried to escape but turned instead to confront her pursuers. Elsewhere (Jacoby *et al.* 1992: 207–8), I have written at length about a young man's dream in which an apparently omnipotent witch-like mother figure who had incarcerated the dreamer was called to account and had to give up a portion of her omnipotence. This had a very liberating effect on the dreamer's self-esteem and, as a result, on his relationships and interactions.

Such transformations cannot be produced by an act of will, either by the analyst or the patient. Both parties are drawn into a process orchestrated by that agency Jung called the "Self." This becomes especially clear when one views the Self as the "directing center that guides the psychic processes toward wholeness" (Neumann 1962: 287). It manifests itself in the drive toward the formation of the personality, that is, the process of individuation. The task of the analyst, whatever his or her method, is to be an instrument and a facilitating environment for psychic processes in accord with the aims of individuation.

SHAME AND THE PROCESS OF INDIVIDUATION

The process of individuation, a central concern in Jungian psychology, is something the Greek poet Pindar brought to expression some 2500 years ago in his famous aphorism, "Become who you are." Repeatedly, Jung struggled to capture in words what he meant by this idea. The following relatively early definition remains a good one.

> In general, it is the process by which individual beings are formed and differentiated; in particular it is the development of the psychological individual as a being distinct from the general, collective psychology. Individuation, therefore, is a process of differentiation, having for its goal the development of the individual personality . . . Since individuality is a prior psychological and physiological datum, it also expresses itself in psychological ways. Any serious check to individuality, therefore, is an artificial stunting . . . Individuation is practically the same as the development of consciousness out of the original state of identity. It is thus an extension of the sphere of consciousness, an enriching of conscious psychological life.
>
> (Jung 1921: paras. 757–62)

We know that Jung saw the process of individuation as beginning with the crises of midlife and becoming active during the second half of life, after one's ego has become somewhat consolidated and one has more or less accomplished the collective tasks of establishing a profession and raising a family. This conception, in my view, is a generalization based on Jung's personal equation and his own experiences, which he described in his memoirs as a "confrontation with the unconscious" (Jung and Jaffé 1963: 194–225). But if one takes seriously his definition of the process of individuation as "the process by which individual beings are formed and differentiated," then early childhood processes of ego development must also be taken into account along with those taking place during the young adult's quest for identity.

One mandate for psychotherapy derives from Jung's idea that the personality is artificially stunted when the process of its natural unfolding is arrested in some way. Individuality is each human being's endowment, and stunting can occur in all phases of life, for a variety of reasons. But without a doubt the greatest dangers to the unfolding of individuality are present during infancy and early childhood, when the balance of facilitation vs. interference lies so completely in the hands of its caretakers, at whose complete mercy an infant finds itself. Since the interaction patterns acquired at that time often influence self-esteem and the quality of human relationships into the present, it seems important to investigate them in depth; usually this artificial stunting has its roots in these early phases of life.

In analysis or psychotherapy, the client must be given an opportunity to reduce the effect of these interferences and to find an attitude that will facilitate the process of unfolding. A great deal will have been accomplished if analysts simply manage to keep from becoming a hindrance to this process, since they can easily overlook the extent to which they themselves may play into the deep ruts of their patients' interaction patterns. This getting bogged down manifests itself in the so-called "resistance," made up of anxiety, shame and mistrust. Often, it is necessary to spend long phases of the analysis working through defenses and negative transferences, as mentioned before. But when it becomes possible for the analysand to go through new experiences and transformations in line with the process of individuation, the analyst is often amazed at the powers of the psyche that are not subject to conscious control, but are rather signs of something greater within us.

In the process of individuation, the psyche's goal-orientation manifests itself as the search for the "realization of one's wholeness." This goal is at the same time a utopic ideal; in reality there are no individuated persons. Rather, individuation entails achieving the most conscious harmony possible between the ego and the powers of the unconscious, which originate in the Self and aim at centering the personality as a whole. Jung also emphasized that the goal of individuation is important "only as an idea." For him, the essential thing was "the *opus* which leads to the goal: that is the goal of a lifetime" (Jung 1946: para. 400). The following acknowledgement of Jung's is relevant to our topic:

> Individuation has two principal aspects: in the first place it is an internal and subjective process of integration, and in the second it is an equally indispensable process of objective relationship.
>
> (Jung 1946: para. 448)

The changing interactions between the ego and the inner figures of the unconscious stand in a mutual relationship with the outer figures of our social reality. Human beings are social creatures, even if they become less dependent on others for validation and self-esteem as they become more integrated and individuated. Having experienced this transformation, I will be more able to affirm my own nature. I may also be in a better position to trust my own "inner voice" when it tells me whether I am living in attunement with my authentic nature.

But what does all this have to do with shame-anxiety and susceptibility to shame? Experientially, quite a lot, since greater self-confidence also means greater freedom in relation to others – whether they are real figures or figures of fantasy. In other words, old fixated interaction patterns can become more pliant and the threshold of shame more flexible. The shame-anxiety associated with how I am seen by others becomes less intense and interfering.

There is yet another benefit in cases of favorable development: the tension is eased between one's wishful fantasy of who one would like to be and one's perception of who one is in reality. At the same time, the aspiration toward a certain perfection energizes the individuation process; the attempt to fulfill the demands of the ego ideal provides a needed motivation. In my opinion one of Jung's most important insights was his distinction between perfection and completeness or wholeness. For example, he wrote that whoever aspires to perfection "must *suffer* from the opposite of his intentions for the sake of completeness" (Jung 1951: para. 123). Perfection excludes all that is shadowy, disturbing, and imperfect, whereas completeness or wholeness must, by definition, include all that is dark, shadowy, and imperfect. As a result, there is bound to be considerable tension between my drive toward perfection and my acceptance of the reality of my being, with its particular shadows and flaws. Indulging in unqualified self-satisfaction will result in a condition of soulless boredom. The feelings of shame, inferiority, and even guilt that surface in such a lifestyle must be taken as signals from the deeper Self that the process of life and individuation is blocked. On the other hand, only by accepting my limitations and consciously enduring my impotencies and inadequacies can I confine my overgrown sense of shame and guilt to its normal guardian function. A course of psychotherapy in which some aspect of the individuation process comes to fruition may help to ease some of the tension between my wish for perfection and my acceptance of the inadequacy of the real me. It may increase the possibility that I may achieve a livable balance time and again.

This is where shame, as a guardian of human dignity, appears to play an important role. In this, I am thinking primarily of that form of shame that Aristotle associated with things of pure truth. Of course we are unable to know with any certainty what "pure truth" is all about. At best we can say that it stands in contrast to the many forms of artificiality and sham that are a part of our lives. All we can do is attempt to gain a sense of our inner truth, to rediscover it again and again, and whenever possible, remain faithful to it. This is a question of ethical conduct, but it is also the essence of the individuation process and of the process by which we establish a relationship to that which is greater within us (see also Beebe 1992). Shame, in the final analysis, should be seen as a guardian of this inner truth, that sounds a disturbing alarm whenever we stray from or avoid that truth.

In practice, one must always ask the question of what meaning feelings of shame may have in each individual situation. On the one hand it is possible to interpret such feelings as serious warning signals from the deep Self that should motivate us to ask ourselves: is there really a reason for me to be ashamed of certain aspects of my attitude or behavior? Am I failing to live in sufficient accord with the deeper concerns of the Self? Could this be a message from God, so to speak, attempting to alert me to such facts? On the other hand, such feelings could just as easily stem from a neurotic susceptibility to shame and point to a lack of self-esteem, an incapacity to accept myself as I am. In other words, they may signal that the tension between the ego and the ego-ideal is for various reasons much too great.

In the end, it is essential that analysts ally themselves with those parts of the analysand that are aiming to satisfy the deeper needs of his or her nature, even if these parts should express themselves in a symptom such as shame. In practice, both possibilities should be considered, as it would not only be presumptuous but therapeutically counterproductive if an analyst were to affirm various manifestations of shame before analytically exploring whether or not these had been produced by some demeaning, shaming inner figure. In such a case, the analyst would also risk confirming the undercutting influence of these figures instead of using interpretation to relativize it. Often, the persons from the analysand's childhood who contributed to the formation of these interaction patterns failed to create a facilitating environment for processes intended by the Self, creating one of obstruction instead. As a result, the analysand grew up not being able to rely on his or her feelings, especially when called on to evaluate his or her own self with its impulses, fantasies, and actions. It is as if there were no inner compass. Sometimes a person will feel ashamed and even guilty about essentially constructive impulses. In such cases, it is as if the Self were "overshadowed" (Asper 1993), i.e. the tendencies originating in the Self were experienced as negative and shameful, when actually they would have been crucial for the development of adequate self-esteem, and ultimately, for individuation. Here the task of analysis is to help the patient re-evaluate his or her values.

THE SNOW WHITE SYNDROME: AN EXAMPLE FROM ANALYTIC PRACTICE

I would like to conclude my comments on the "overshadowed Self" with an illustration from my practice that closely follows an archetypal pattern vividly expressed in the fairy-tale, "Snow White." The fairy tale can be seen as a collective, archetypal background for my client's personal situation.

The tale itself deals with the fatal rejection and poisoning of a daughter by a stepmother/witch. In general, the poison of rejection can pit destructive feelings of shame and guilt against vital life impulses so that one experiences one's strivings for individuation as shameful and presumptuous or simply bad. Under the influence of this poison, the values that nature contributes to the process of self-formation are overshadowed, as it were, and slanderously turned into negatives.

My case history concerns an attractive 35-year-old woman whose mother had still been very young and apparently very beautiful when she gave birth to her. The father must have left the family shortly afterwards, but the mother always told my client that her father had died. As she found out later, this was just one of many lies that she was brought up on. "Ms. X," as I will call her, also remembers that her mother always wanted to be the center of attention and that she desperately needed to win the admiration of everybody in her environment. Furthermore, my patient remembers that she herself had admired her charming mother tremendously and that she was obliged to please her by obeying her every command and fulfilling her every wish. At much too early an age, she had had to adapt to her mother's needs, performing the role of admirer and even servant in order to be sure of mother's love and attention. From very early on she did household chores for her mother and tried to read mother's wishes from the look in her eye. She had to hold a kind of magic mirror before her mother that constantly confirmed, "You are the fairest in the land." The kind of mirroring my patient received in return was, "You are the best and dearest – as long as you admire me as the fairest in the land and remain a part of me by serving my needs." In Kohut's terms, the daughter had to function as a "mirroring self-object" to her mother – instead of the other way around as it should have been.

But things between mother and daughter became pretty rough once this arrangement began to shift. When at puberty my patient began herself to look attractive, her mother did not hesitate to put her down with tactless, humiliating remarks. By then the mother had remarried and surrounded herself with other admirers, whom she was determined to keep away from her daughter. This was clearly not done in a spirit of maternal solicitude, but rather of envy and rivalry. She was not entirely successful, however. As is so often the case in such situations, the stepfather made secret advances toward the girl, grotesquely abusing his position of power. Fearing her mother's wrath, the daughter had no choice but to keep the matter to herself.

As soon as she had developed the first signs of puberty, she must have become vaguely conscious that her mother was indeed rejecting her and pushing her away. But she could not allow herself to feel outright anger at her parents, and so instead felt deeply ashamed of herself, a bad and worthless person. Her one chance for survival lay in the possibility of taking refuge with "the seven dwarfs behind the mountains."[7] She was searching for meaning and God through her imagination and dreams. Of course, she also felt intense longing for love and an exchange of affection. Being attractive, she did later on as an adult have several relationships with men. Yet it was in just this area that mother's poisoning was most effective. No relationship survived for any length of time; for one reason or another they all fell apart.

This problematic state of affairs is symbolized in the fairy tale by the vivid image of the red half of the apple that the witch-mother had poisoned. The queen, disguised as a farmer's wife, offers this half of the apple to Snow White, and the girl cannot resist taking a bite. The apple is a fruit of love as well as of knowledge. Biting into the red half signifies getting in touch with blood as life-force, passion, and sensuality. It is maturation toward such love and passion that is poisoned and prohibited by the envious witch-mother.

The constellation is one we come across all too frequently. Mothers who make a display of their own innocence in matters of sex and love – who bite the white part of the apple – often prevent their daughters from having relationships with members of the male sex and to sexuality altogether. "Take care, my child, men only want one thing, and we are above that," they seem to hint at every occasion, whether appropriate or not – often motivated by their own repressed sexuality. I have also seen that mothers who are dissatisfied with their marriages often take their daughters into their confidence at too early an age, crying about their unhappiness, for which they blame their husbands, and accusing men in general of being aggressive, bestial, or utterly unfaithful. In doing this, they are biting into the white part of the apple and giving the poisoned red part to their daughters. The poison may instill in the daughters an unconscious fear and rejection of all matters of love and a repression of their own instinctive side, which longs for relationship. Often one can find in such mothers an unconscious envy of their daughters' femininity.

During the analysis, I realized that Ms. X's basic problem was that she was compelled to experience her own impulses, as well as everything else inside her, as bad, unreliable, and shameful. However, with time she did become more aware of her own inner life, needs, and desires. Previously, she had been aware chiefly of the needs of those around her; she obligingly had been a part of their fantasies, as if she were being lived by them. The new awareness caused her to severely deprecate herself, to condemn herself for having resentments and negative, critical feelings toward many of her friends. She also came to recognize her envy and jealousy, especially toward women friends whom she had been mothering. Again, one could see that she had grown up unconsciously evaluating herself according to a standard by which being good meant acting as a mirror or a servant for her wonderful mother. By contrast, all of her impulses toward autonomy, all her own needs, and her strivings for self-esteem were bad. In analysis, her stated intention was to take steps in the process of finding herself, of individuating. Thus her newfound ability to entertain negative, critical thoughts and resentments were extremely important attempts by her deeper Self to define her own boundaries over and against people who had so often used her as a kind of trash can in which to dump their "shit." Still, an inner, negative mother challenged her right to set such boundaries and condemned her with feelings of guilt and shame if she were to do anything that appeared the least bit egoistic or negative. So her envy of her mother was not only natural, it was quite understandable; to admit it and, if possible, accept it was essential for her healing and self-realization. Because of her extreme sensitivity, she must have known as a child that she was a victim of her mother's envy, but any such knowledge had long ago been repressed in view of the great risk of losing mother's love. None-theless, in analysis, the effects of the envy came to the fore.

Ms. X was shocked to be confronted with the resurfacing of this sense of having been a victim of her mother's envy. This reminds us of that passage in "Snow White" in which Snow White's coffin is lifted to be carried away, gets dropped and the jolt dislodges the poisoned piece of apple from her throat. This jolt in the analysis motivated Ms. X to spit up various poisoned thoughts and feelings, and this helped towards re-evaluating her distorted inner values and gradually to admit and accept her true feelings. Most importantly, she had to gain trust in the value of her inner world and Self. The "little dwarfs" helped a great deal by crafting dreams that accom-panied and supported this process. For example, one night she dreamed that she saw a coffin on a hill. Suddenly she heard the voice of a woman from inside the coffin. Shuddering to think of the experiences that this woman must have endured, she felt an urge to run away.

The dream provided the opportunity to speak of the "Snow White syndrome." The coffin episode in the fairy tale also marks the appearance of the prince, the son of the king, who "loves her better than all the world." In many fairy tales a female hero is redeemed by means of a prince's love. It is the love which has a redemptive effect. Psychologically, one could say that in the course of a process of self-discovery a loving and caring attitude toward one's own being has become possible. A deep love-experience with a real partner may of course have a redeeming quality, furthering one's awareness of the richness of one's own inner resources. In analysis, the experience of the analyst's empathic care may help to awaken a new attitude toward one's own being, modifying the destructive negativity of introjected parental figures. But neither empathy nor love can bring about any change unless there is an inner readiness for change. Therefore, the loving prince should be seen as an inner figure that symbolizes a loving and affirming care for one's own being and the transformation of a negative interaction pattern.

But such a transformation was still quite a ways off for Ms. X. Her growing awareness of the ongoing influence of her early childhood pattern remained a source of overwhelming shame. Until this stage of her analysis, she had lived with the illusory conviction of having been a happy child, pleased with her fascinating mother. The humiliating aspects of her childhood and early youth and the dishonest assumptions and outright lies in the home atmosphere had to be repressed. They provoked too much shame, shedding a bad light on her family situation. Again and again during the analysis, she rose to protect and defend her mother. She said that her mother wasn't so bad after all, and besides, this was the only mother – the only family – she had. Yet at the same time she did not feel she belonged there. In reality, she felt guilty the moment she caught herself harboring bad thoughts about her mother or her stepfather – even though

109

this same man had been driven out of the house by her mother. Unresolved parental ties often exercise their influence by means of guilt. Guilt prohibits one from asserting oneself and striving to be free of the expectations and sensibilities of one's parents.

At the same time these new awarenesses provoked overwhelming shame in Ms. X. She was ashamed of her background, of coming from a family in which lies, intrigues, and mean quarrels were the order of the day. She felt soiled by these realities and disgusted to be a part of such a family. Now her striving for spiritual values seemed to her nothing more than an attempt to purify herself of so much soil. Ms. X thus increasingly found herself in a serious shame–guilt dilemma. Whenever she was flooded with shame about her childhood environment, she felt accusations and hate toward her mother, which caused her profound guilt. Her guilt in turn forbade feelings of shame about her family, for such shame would expose her mother to deprecating judgments. Yet as time went on, the shame became more and more intolerable. At times this conflict was so overwhelming that she fell into depressions characterized by heavy self-doubt.

Naturally these conflicts also came up in the transference. She doubted whether I could really tolerate someone so bad and degraded as she, and she wanted to keep me as far away as possible from her dirt. Perhaps the poison was so contagious that I would not want anything to do with her. But at the same time she hated me for putting down her mother – though in reality I did nothing of the kind. She had clearly made enormous progress when she could finally speak about such resentments. One must appreciate what it meant for her to overcome her old, accustomed attitude of over-compliance and to risk the withdrawal of my love by genuinely standing up for herself. Because on the whole, arising out of fear of losing my interest and care, she tried her best to burden me as little as possible, to tune into me, and bring to the analysis material that would be interesting and stimulating for me. Thus, as expected, her early childhood interaction pattern manifested itself in the therapeutic relationship. In part, this pattern expressed itself as a capacity to respond sensitively to and satisfy the needs of others. Indeed, she had developed an extraordinary capacity for empathy.

As for my counter-transference, I usually felt very spirited in her presence and looked forward to the sessions. Often I was surprised by the precision of my interpretations and the depth of the insights that came from our being together. This counter-transferential reaction naturally raised certain questions. Was I responding to an unconscious seduction on her part? Was she animating me, evoking my "anima," so that I would feel wonderful in her presence – so that I would love her in return? Was she holding a magic mirror before me as she had done for her mother, enabling me to see myself as the fairest – or at least the best and brightest – in all the land? It was important for me to remain aware of these aspects of our interaction. But it was just as important not to fixate on her arts of seduction, which sprang from an inner need. If I had, I might have forfeited an important opportunity for a therapeutic new beginning. For I became aware that our mutual fit really was based on a common wavelength, a *coniunctio* in the symbolic language of the alchemists – or, to use Stern's words, a deep encounter in the "intersubjective domain." Therein lay a creative possibility for developmental processes.

Often it struck me that I seemed a bit too smart in our sessions, as if I was doing too much lecturing. One day I realized that I was explaining things to her that she knew as well as I. And yet she admired my "wisdom" nevertheless. This led me to realize that she had developed an intense idealizing transference toward me. This idealization had two different functions in her psychic economy. The first was defensive. By experiencing me as wonderful and elevated she could defend herself against other, not so pleasant feelings that she simultaneously harbored in connection to father figures. In this way, she attempted to protect our relationship from an excess of ambivalence. Idealization was at the same time her psyche's creative attempt to constellate a loving prince, an emotionally reliable and related masculine figure such as she had never before experienced.

When I fell into lecturing her about connections that she must have long been aware of – which she skillfully drew out of me by playing the naive and curious little girl – I realized that this game was highly important for the development of her self-esteem. She needed to hear me confirm what she already knew, otherwise she could not really own it. Her self-knowledge was constantly threatened, as it were, by the magic spells and poisoned comb of the inner witch. She was not permitted to have this knowledge, because she was not worthy of it – not worthy of understanding her inner situation and the value of her being.

In reality, I was repeatedly moved by her highly differentiated potential for insight and the deep strivings of her psyche toward individuation. Thus it was obvious that I believed in her possibilities and the rich substance of her soul. She also called me her "bank" in which she could safely deposit her valuables. This was an important image for her, as she really was never sure of her value and was in danger of losing it at any moment. Of course, I often questioned myself and tried to be sure that, motivated by the illusions of my own counter-transference, I was not idealizing her. It was important to keep this possibility in mind, for had I done so, I would have withdrawn some valuables from her "account" to use for my own purposes. As her bank, it was crucial that I be as trustworthy as possible, for everything depended on her having reliable access to what she had deposited there. It was therefore important that our mutual consent, even our harmony and oneness, should remain intact and unclouded by the least shadow of doubt.

Of course, such a paradisiacal oneness is not possible. In fact, it is important that some disappointments and misunderstandings occur so that they can be worked through. And indeed, in the course of analysis the following event took place. Ms. X called me one day in order to postpone an appointment. It was difficult for me to find another time, having given someone else the last free hour shortly before. Thus, without thinking, I remarked, "It is a shame you did not call earlier." That was enough to provoke a crisis of trust between us.

Only retrospectively did I become aware of my lack of empathy on the phone. I should have known, I later realized, how difficult it had been for her to telephone and request something for herself. It was obvious that my reaction felt to her like a reproach, conveying all at once rejection, withdrawal of love, lack of empathy, and a rupture of our mutual understanding. At the same time, she felt ashamed at having been so thrown off-balance by such a trivial little incident. Thus it was essential that both of us find empathy and understanding for the child within her who felt unloved and rejected whenever it expressed the slightest need or wish.

Basically, the aim of the analysis was for Ms. X to come to believe in the prizing and attention she got from me and others close to her, to nurture herself by taking it in, and finally to internalize it as a caring attitude toward herself. As long as she experienced herself as just a piece of shit (as she often called herself) the discrepancy between her own sense of self-esteem and others' opinion of her was too great. A short dream seemed to signal the onset of a decisive transformation. In it, she allows a man to look intensely into her eyes. Then she realizes that this look is waking up and inspiring something in her.

Shame usually prevents such intense eye contact; after all, to feel someone looking deeply into one's eyes often causes embarrassment. Thus the dream shed a certain light on the transference situation. Perhaps it indicated that she was beginning to accept some of the ways that I prized her, and that part of her being was thus coming to life. Indeed, this awakening coincided with the beginning of a change in her image of men.

Toward the end of the analysis came a dream that made a powerful impression on her. She sees me, her analyst, sitting in the middle of a round, wood-paneled hall. The atmosphere is radiant and warm. I am sitting peacefully at a writing desk engrossed in study or meditation. Next to me on the table are a set of keys that permits access to a network of side-halls lined with bookshelves. The library contains volumes in which the treasures of all of Western culture have been set down. I, the analyst, possess the keys; one has to come to me to ask for them. Yet I seem to provide them in a generous way.

The dream expresses an enormous idealization indeed: I am seated in the center, holding the keys to all of Western cultural knowledge – a realm that lay outside of her family disgrace and in which she had always taken refuge. While naturally flattering, such an idealization can also be embarrassing to an analyst, evoking certain feelings of shame as a defense against his own grandiosity. Yet this dream-image was so clearly an idealization having little to do with my real human limitations that I was not about to identify with it.

Here I must reiterate how important it is for analysts to separate themselves from the various roles and meanings they take on as transference figures in the patient's world. In Ms. X's dream, I was a highly symbolic figure created by her soul for the purpose of helping her to individuate. Sometimes the analyst has to carry such an image for an extended period of time. But an image is not the same as a real person; it merely functions as an instrument for the realization of deeper aspects of the Self. Ms. X was now far enough along in her process that we could interpret the dream on the subjective level; in other words, we could discuss whether the figure in the library, personified as me, could not actually portray her own liberal access to knowledge. It seemed crucial to me that the keys to knowledge should not remain in my hands but become tools for her own use. In time, she should not need me to tell her what she already knew, what she was unable to own or live without my affirmation. Indeed, the sucessful transfer of these keys would become the goal of the analysis.

CONCLUDING REMARKS ON PSYCHOTHERAPY

I hope that this detailed vignette from my practice illustrates how closely shame-anxieties are bound up with disturbances in self-esteem, and their work to impair the self-realization process. The Snow White motif is common among people who suffer from such problems, created when one's self-esteem and even one's sense of birthright are poisoned by a rejecting attitude on the part of the maternal figure – indeed, sometimes the paternal figure as well. Like Snow White, persons suffering from such wounds cannot free themselves from the poisoning effect of inner figures; they readily identify with them and believe their deprecating attitudes. Thus the evil queen is unquestionably right when she labels one's every attempt to gain self-confidence or self-worth as a shameful presumption. Often the evil queen takes the form of a relentless grandiose self – the fairest in the land – whose unrealizable demands for perfection make one feel perennially small and unworthy.

Psychotherapy must set its sights on a successful enough re-examination of this distorted value system. Because such a twisted self-valuation stems from interaction patterns established early in life, the distortion is usually anchored deep in the personality. That is why the analytic process may suffer repeated setbacks in such cases. Again and again, the smallest triggers may cause the analysand to surrender to the power of negative complexes with their old, familiar interaction patterns. The therapist's empathic stability is a vital element in this process, for it keeps the patient from feeling forsaken amidst these ups and downs. Besides, the analysand fears nothing so much as rejection, even if he or she seems to be constantly provoking it from the therapist. What the analyst needs above all else in this prolonged process is a therapeutic attitude like the one C.G. Jung referred to so often, calling upon the famous words of an alchemist. Though it may have become a cliché by now, this alchemical saying is still valid for us, for it reminds us that, finally, the work can only succeed *deo concedente* – "with the help of God."

APPENDIX

CONCEPTS OF THE EGO AND THE SELF: A COMPARISON

Whether it is possible to work Daniel Stern's hypotheses into existing models of the psyche remains to be seen. One might even ask if this is necessary. Isn't it possible to let each theory stand independently of the other – in spite of the perennial human need for integration? Although in this book I have not dedicated myself to a comparison of various concepts of the self, I do not wish to end it without making some attempt to relate those findings of infant research that seem important to me to the better-known psychoanalytic views – especially Jungian ones.

Much in Stern's work has not really been thought through yet, particularly the decisive question of how the verbal domain of the infant's sense of self relates to the "lost global experience" of the pre- or non-verbal sense of self. What is the significance of this global experience? How can Stern be sure that before the verbal phase (fifteen to eighteen months old), the infant's communication with its mother, which seems so real and adaptive, is not interwoven with fantasies? We are still quite ignorant about what takes place in the psyche of the pre-verbal infant. And, to be fair, Stern does not claim to know, though his hypotheses are based on marvelously refined studies of infant behavior. Thus it is with some justification that he speaks of the difference between the "observed" and the "clinical" infant, drawing our attention to the uneasy relationship between the experimental approach of infant research and the clinical, psychoanalytic methods that attempt to reconstruct early childhood from analysands' memories and transferences. Stern wishes to establish a dialogue between these two disciplines that will be fruitful for both. And he is in a good position to do so, having devoted himself not only to research in developmental psychology but to the practice of psychoanalysis.

How are we to conceive of this pre-verbal wholeness of experience that Stern writes about? The child in the phase of the verbal sense of self mourns the wholeness of experience that it has lost forever. Margaret Mahler described this pre-verbal wholeness as a phase in which the infant, living in an illusion of symbiotic unity with its mother, feels omnipotent (Mahler *et al.* 1975: 43ff). Like Stern, Mahler observed a "sobering" of the child (the so-called "rapprochement crisis"), which she believed resulted when the child had become separated enough from the mother and the original symbiosis to realize that he or she is not omnipotent but small and dependent. While Stern speaks of "global experience," Mahler speaks of feelings of "unlimited omnipotence." This brings up several questions, possibly unanswerable: how is this wholeness-of-experience like Fordham's "primary self" or Jung's hypothesis of the Self as a symbol of wholeness? Is this wholeness-of-experience the result only of real interactions with the mother or does it also spring from the experience of an unconscious inner world that the child only begins to perceive in the verbal phase? Isn't "being in the wholeness" also an experience of unlimited omnipotence? Do infants have an innate sense of self that already experiences wholeness or omnipotence? Could an infant have an intimation of such an experience without knowing it? I suspect it could, but that only after the onset of the verbal phase and the birth of reflective consciousness does it link up earlier, unconscious experiences with inner ideas or representations. The "paradise" of wholeness or unitary reality (Neumann) only becomes conscious after it has been lost. All the same, the phase of omnipotence postulated by Mahler and many psychoanalysts seems significant to the extent that it is related to psychological symptoms that, in adults, suggest a grandiose self.

Furthermore, I would like to look at the difference between the psychoanalytic view that the infant lives in a symbiotic union with its mother and Stern's view, which emphasizes the infant's dependence on a "self-regulating other." Is the difference really so fundamental, I wonder, or is it simply a question of where the observer places the accent? Stern dismisses the notion of a primary symbiosis, believing rather that the infant enters life with a subjective sense of self, i.e., the feeling that "I am in my own, separate body." Fordham shares this perspective (1976: 11ff). The influence and presence of another person (the mother) does, however, effect changes in this sense of self. But then what is symbiosis? It seems to me that subjective experience takes place even in states of symbiosis: I feel as if mother and I are one heart and soul. In my view, a subjective "I" is present if only in rudimentary form even during experiences of symbiosis – indeed, at all times except perhaps in certain schizophrenic or depersonalized states. Naturally, there are states of fusion and confusion with significant others. Jung called these "unconscious identity" or "mystical participation" (1921: CW 6: 821 and 856), and Melanie Klein proposed the term "projective identification" for them (Segal 1964). And yet this does not invalidate the subjective experience that "it is I" who experiences the other as a part of myself, or myself as a part of the other. An underlying sense of self remains intact even if mutual influence has made the boundaries between us quite permeable.

And yet I agree that the quality of subjective experience may vary greatly, depending on whether I find myself imaginatively at one with a more powerful other, or just dependent on others for their self-regulating functions. It seems probable to me that infants oscillate between these two types of experience. Yet in both cases, the experience is strongly affected by the degree to which parent and child can attune themselves to each other and develop between them a relatively good fit. For the time being, it remains an open question whether these two types of experience – "I am dependent on a self-regulating other," and "as part of a powerful other, I am myself powerful" – occur in developmental succession or more or less simultaneously. In any case, they correspond to two different basic feeling states that can also appear later in adult life.

For example, consider the analytical phenomenon whereby, for prolonged periods, analysands see themselves as strong and relatively invulnerable because they feel fused with the analyst and carried by the wisdom of Jungian (or Freudian or Existential) psychology. At other times, this same emotional dependence on their analyst for psychic equilibrium seems to them a forfeiture of self worth: "I can not even deal with my own life: what a disgrace!"

Naturally, the views of C.G. Jung are of particular importance in any comparison of concepts of ego and Self. Before continuing with my own commentary, I would like to remind my reader of Jung's distinction between the ego and the Self:

> By ego I understand a complex of ideas which constitutes the centre of my field of consciousness and appears to possess a high degree of continuity and identity. Hence I also speak of an *ego-complex*. The ego-complex is as much a content as a condition of *consciousness*, for a psychic element is conscious inasmuch as it is related to my ego-complex. But inasmuch as the ego is only the centre of my field of consciousness, it is not identical with the totality of my psyche, being merely one complex among other complexes. I therefore distinguish between the ego and the self, since the ego is only the subject of my consciousness, while the self is the subject of my total psyche, which also includes the unconscious. In this sense the self would be an ideal entity which embraces the ego.

(Jung 1926: 810)

First let us consider the ego, in regard to which Jung's hypothesis is of particular interest – namely, that the ego-complex is both a content of consciousness and a precondition of consciousness. The ego is thus the necessary condition for something's becoming conscious: "a psychic element is conscious inasmuch as it is related to my ego-complex" (Jung 1921: 706). But at the same time, the ego-complex is a content of consciousness. This implies that I can make myself a content and thus an object of my self-reflective awareness. Jung's definition has two sides, corresponding roughly to a subjective and an objective way of perceiving. Each of these needs to be distinguished from the other. Subjectively, I experience myself as the continuous center of conscious will, action, and intention, and as the receiver of impressions. These intentions are usually directed at other persons and things of the outer world, that is, at objects. It is from objects as well that I receive impressions. But I can also objectify myself such that I become a content of my own consciousness – what, in most cases, we would call a "self-image" or "self-representation."

It seems to me that we can only speak of consciousness in a Jungian sense as linked with the ego-complex once the stage of the verbal sense of self has been reached, enabling one to make oneself the object of one's own observation and judgment. In this case, what we mean by consciousness is the capacity for reflection based on the opposites of subject and object, good and evil, masculine and feminine, etc. Without knowledge of the opposites, conscious differentiation with its comparisons and contrasts would not be possible.

This brings us back to the myth of paradise, in which the original instance of shame is the result of an awareness of the opposites. Growth of consciousness means "loss of paradise." In other words, shame in its fullest sense first appears along with the verbal sense of self. Only then can one see one's own person "from the outside" or can one's subjective sense of self relate to the image one carries of oneself. Or, in Jung's words, only then does a self-image form as a content of the ego-complex. As mentioned before, children who are just beginning to speak refer to themselves in the third person, the same way that their significant others speak of them: "Jackie," or "Tony" is nice, bad, tired, etc. It is as if they were looking at themselves from the outside, seeing and judging themselves with the eyes of significant others. This capacity is rooted in pre-verbal experiences of "self with others," memory-traces of earlier interactional patterns which have now become partially accessible to verbal expression and to the kind of consciousness whose center Jung called the ego. However, it takes a while for this verbalizable representation of oneself to fuse with the subjective sense of self and become integrated as a feeling of identity.

What does it mean that the ego is a precondition of consciousness? Certainly the ego could never fulfill this condition without possessing a "high degree of continuity and identity" (Jung 1955: 706). Of course, temporal continuity and identity are existential categories that can only be lived, however much contemplation and philosophical thought they have inspired. They are also basic feelings rooted in what Stern called "the domain of the core self," – something that is largely, though not exclusively, equivalent to the body-self.

"The ego," wrote Jung, "ostensibly the thing we know most about, is in fact a highly complex affair full of unfathomable obscurities" (Jung 1955: 129). The basis of ego-centered consciousness – the root of consciousness, as it were – reaches down into the unconscious. Its core is an active energy that arranges and organizes the process of self-development. Jung called this hypothetical center "the Self"[8] and stressed that every effort should be made to maintain a relationship between the ego and Self. The Self is the very source of our creative energies; one might even say that it creates the human being and directs the development of consciousness. It is also involved in the organization of the various "domains of the sense of self" as described by Stern, a process which leads finally to a mature self-awareness.

Three theses proposed by Stern seem to be of particular relevance to these basic Jungian tenets:

1) The domain of the emergent self in the first phase of infancy is the foundational experience for all creative human possibilities.
2) Stern wrote of the core self: "Somehow [!] the infant registers the objective experience with self-regulating others as a subjective experience" (Stern 1985: 104). What principle of organization makes it possible for such a central process to "somehow" take place?
3) For Stern, the emergence of the "domain of the verbal self" coincides with the feeling of a loss of wholeness. This development recalls the birth of the ego, as Jung defined it – as the center of a consciousness that has become capable of reflection. From there the knowledge of the opposites and of one's personal distinctness over and against the unconscious grows.

Erich Neumann distinguished between two forms of consciousness. In his view, the reflecting consciousness of the verbal domain correspond to the "solar" or "patriarchal" principle. Just as the sunlight enables us to discern the outlines of things, the borders between illuminated and shadowed areas, solar consciousness strives for clear definitions and logical connections. This corresponds to "patriarchal" consciousness, whose symbolic center is the head (Neumann 1954: 218).

On the other side is the "lunar" or "matriarchal" consciousness. Like the moon with its silvery glow, this consciousness does not delineate the contours of individual objects but envelops all things in its embracing mood. For this reason, the moon has become a central image of lyrical poetry, from Goethe to Claudius to Li-tai-pe. Lunar consciousness is one that is open to feelings and intuitions that do not easily lend themselves to definite verbal form. Matriarchal consciousness is symbolized by the heart.

Matriarchal consciousness experiences the dark and mysterious process of growing comprehension as something in which the self functions as a totality.

(Neumann 1954: 224)

Even if Neumann's psychology of "archetypal stages of development" put more emphasis on passive containment in the earliest phase of the infant (an emphasis that puts him largely in agreement with Mahler), it seems to me that his description of "lunar-matriarchal" consciousness strongly corresponds with Stern's description of the pre-verbal sense of self and its experiences of relatedness (Neumann 1988: 11). The theory that the growth of consciousness is a psychic process "guided" by the Self does not necessarily contradict the observation that the various stages of development unfold via interactions with a partner in which the infant's self plays an active role. Michael Fordham, another proponent of the Jungian view, also took this into account in his theory of the "primary self," which de-integrates and re-integrates in concert with the mother (Fordham 1969; Jacoby 1990).

To sum up: We have to distinguish between the psychoanalytic idea of the self, which is largely equivalent with the self-representation, or self-image and the Jungian Self. In Jungian terms, this self-representation or self-image would be comparable to a content of the ego-complex. But we must emphasize that the self-image is only partially the object of conscious reflection; unconscious factors influence it as well. Theoretically, however, it is possible to bring large parts of one's self-image to conscious awareness; indeed, this is often the goal of a therapeutic analysis.

By calling the ego-complex a precondition of consciousness, Jung presented us with an insoluble riddle. What, finally, does this precondition consist of, and what is it based upon? With the help of science, we have gained increasingly refined insights into the laws of nature and the mysteries of the human brain. Modern infant research in particular has made significant contributions to this knowledge, which I have drawn from a great deal in writing this book. Yet an understanding of the essence of nature and life in its physical, psychological, and intellectual manifestations continues to elude our grasp. Nor have we yet identified the central source of information, which guides psychic growth and the process of becoming conscious. We are still struggling to understand what, finally, the condition of consciousness is all about. Nevertheless, we can scarcely avoid positing some central agent in the unconscious that structures and organizes our psyches.

The Self Jung writes about is thus a hypothetical central agent that makes possible the development of consciousness and governs the entire personality. The ego, on the other hand, is just a part of the total personality, which consists of both consciousness and the unconscious. However, it is the precondition, the *conditio sine qua non*, for our being able to experience the world and see ourselves.

Fundamentally imperceptible, the Self may manifest in an endless number of symbols – often of a numinous cast – appearing from the unconscious. According to Jung, the symbol is "the best possible formulation of a relatively *unknown* thing which for that reason cannot be more clearly or characteristically represented" (Jung 1921: 815). The appearance of the Self in the form of a symbol is a harbinger of unknown energies, and may thus suggest and invite an opening to the dimension of religion.

These complex ideas might become more lucid if I made use of religious terminology. That is to say, God created each child as it is, bequeathing to it its inherent (or genetic) predispositions and potentialities. God then proceeds to guide the child's development – or, if you will, its God-given destiny. Thus the development/destiny of the child is a manifestation of God's power; a Higher Authority orders each child's biopsychic life.

At the same time God is a concept that can only be expressed symbolically, since the Deity Itself – assuming It exists – can never be perceived in Its true form. Hence, individuals experience God's effect existentially when they perceive forces within themselves and limitations imposed upon them that they have no control over, but that nonetheless play a crucial role in molding their destiny. At the same time, some concept or image of the Divine spontaneously imprints itself upon their psyches. Thus, we might say that a mysterious divine spark is at work within us, causing us to generate ideas and images about God and the works of God which are necessarily of a symbolic nature. So much for my attempt to bring various perspectives and views of the self into a possible correlation.

NOTES

1 This collective shame is only partially linked to personal concerns about having an ugly or disgusting body.
2 However, more recent findings by infant researchers should be added in regard to this hypothesis. By the age of 2–3 months, children recognize the face of their mothers, even when it expresses a variety of affects and moods. Infants thus understand the identity of a face even when its appearance is altered (Stern 1985: 87f). Of course the caretaker's emotional state and how he expresses it greatly influences the child's emotions.
3 However, this does not necessarily mean that the first signs of shame-affects manifest in the first two or three months of life.
4 In the place of the word "conscience" I would substitute "premature, inner self-observing function," since it is not only a matter of being punished but also of being shamed.
5 It should be added that even today some European and American mothers swear to this "health practice," which Parin and Morgenthaler have also observed among the Agni tribe of Africa (Parin *et al.* 1971). These authors gave their book on the ethno-psychoanalysis of the tribe the provocative title, *Fear Thy Neighbor as Thyself*. The Agni are a rich, noble warrior people with a long and proud tradition. But tribal life is dominated by universal distrust. Anxiety and rage can break out at any time from behind a façade of rigid, noble etiquette. The Agni do not enter into long, committed love relationships, and one of their most significant sayings is, "Follow your heart and you will die" (Parin *et al.* 1971: 562; cf. Jacoby 1985: 64–5).
6 In my opinion, this fantasy had as little to do with psychotic delusion as his idea of being observed had to do with full-blown paranoid.
7 Dwarfs have many symbolic meanings in mythology and folklore. They are always connected with nature and Mother Earth, and were viewed in antiquity as helpers of the Great Mother known as *kabirs* or *daktyloi*, meaning "fingers." Thus, they have a phallic-creative aspect. Often they were depicted as smiths, sages, inventors of musical rhythms, and magicians. They worked inside the earth, searching in mountain caves for gold, bronze and other metals, and guarding treasures there. According to Jung, they represent creative forces in the unconscious.
8 Modern psychoanalysis has proposed the notion of a "superordinate ego," a construct partially congruent with the Jungian idea of the "self." The superordinate ego "always strives for the preservation of the organism by resolution of conflicts and favoring ongoing developmental processes" (R. and G. Blanck 1986: 34–5).

BIBLIOGRAPHY

Asper, K. (1993) *The Abandoned Child within Losing and Regaining Self-Worth*, New York: Fromm International.

Bächtold-Stäubli, H. (1927) *Handwörterbuch des Deutschen Aberglaubens*, Berlin and Leipzig: De Gruyter.

Beebe, J. (1992) *Integrity in Depth*, College Station: Texas A&M University Press.

Blanck, R. and Blanck, G. (1986) *Beyond Ego Psychology*, New York: Columbia Press.

Blaser, P. and Poeldinger, W. (1967) "Angst als geistesgeschichtliches Phänomen und naturwissenschaftliches Problem," in Kielholz, P. (ed.) *Angst*, pp. 11–36, Basle and Stuttgart: Huber.

Blomeyer, R. (1974) "Aspekte der Persona," *Analytische Psychologie* 5(1): 17–29, Basle: Karger.

Duerr, H. P. (1988) *Nacktheit und Scham*, 3rd edn, Frankfurt a.M.: Suhrkamp.

Eibl-Eibesfeldt, I. (1973) *Der vorprogrammierte Mensch*, Vienna: Molden.

Erikson, E. H. (1950) *Childhood and Society*, New York: Norton.

Fordham, M. (1957) "Notes on the transference," in *Technique in Jungian Analysis*, 1974, pp. 111–51, London: Heinemann.

Fordham, M. (1969) *Children as Individuals*, London: Hodder & Stoughton.

Fordham, M. (1976) *The Self and Autism*, London: Heinemann Medical Books.

Fordham, M. (1986) *Exploration into the Self*, London: Karnac Books.

Freud, A. (1965) *Normality and Pathology in Childhood. Assessments of Development*, New York: International Universities Press.

Freud, S. (1923) "The Ego and the Id," in Strachey, J. (ed.) *The Complete Psychological Works, XIX*, London: Hogarth Press.

Goethe, J. W. von (1873) "Rameau's Neffe, ein Dialog von Diderot," *Gesammelte Werke, 26*, Berlin: Grote'sche Verlagsbuchhandlung.

Gordon, R. (1985) "Big Self and Little Self: Some Reflections," *Journal of Analytical Psychology* 30 (3): 261–71. London: Academic Press.

Gordon, R. (1987) "Masochism: the Shadow Side of the Archetypal Need to Venerate and Worship," *Journal of Analytical Psychology* 32 (3): 227–40. London: Academic Press.

Grimm, J. and Grimm, W. (1960) *Deutsches Wörterbuch*, München: Deutscher Taschenbuchverlag.

Grimm, R. (1972) "Die Paradiesesehe, eine erotische Utopie des Mittelalters," in *Festschrift für W. Mohr* (Göppinger Arbeiten zur Germanistik, 65), Göppingen.

Hartmann, H. (1964) *Essays on Ego-Psychology*, New York: International Universities Press.

Hultberg, P. (1988) "Shame: a Hidden Emotion," *Journal of Analytical Psychology* 33 (2): 109–26. London: Academic Press.

Illies, J. (1971) *Zoologie des Menschen: Entwurf einer Anthropologie*, München: Piper.

Izard, C. E. (1977) *Human Emotions*, New York and London: Plenum Press.

Jacobi, J. (1959) *Complex/Archetype/Symbol in the Psychology of C. G. Jung*, New York: Pantheon Books.

Jacobi, J. (1971) *Die Seelenmaske*, Olten and Freiburg i.Br.: Walter.

Jacobson, E. (1964) *The Self and the Object World*, New York: International Universities Press.

Jacoby, M. (1984) *The Analytic Encounter: Transference and Human Relationship*, Toronto: Inner City Books.

Jacoby, M. (1985) *The Longing for Paradise*, Boston: Sigo Press.

Jacoby, M. (1990) *Individuation and Narcissism: The Psychology of the Self in Jung and Kohut*, London and New York: Routledge.

Jacoby, M., Kast, V. and Riedel, I. (1992) *Witches, Ogres, and the Devil's Daughter*, Boston and London: Shambhala.

Jung, C. G. *The Collected Works*, (CW), edited by H. Read, M. Fordham, and G. Adler, translated by R. F. C. Hull, London: Routledge & Kegan Paul.

Jung, C. G. (1921) *Psychological Types, CW 6*.

Jung, C. G. (1928) *The Relations between the Ego and the Unconscious, CW 7*.

Jung, C. G. (1929) *Problems of Modern Psychotherapy, CW 16*.

Jung, C. G. (1935a) *Principles of Practical Psychotherapy, CW 16*.

Jung, C. G. (1935b) "On the Theory and Practice of Analytical Psychology," *The Tavistock Lectures, CW 18*.

Jung, C. G. (1939) *Psychological Aspects of the Mother Archetype, CW 9i*.

Jung, C. G. (1946) *The Psychology of Transference, CW 16*.

Jung, C. G. (1951) *Aion, CW 9ii*.

Jung, C. G. (1955) *Mysterium Coniunctionis, CW 14*.

Jung, C. G. and Jaffé, A. (1963) *Memories, Dreams, Reflections*, London: Collins, London: Routledge & Kegan Paul.

Kast, V. (1980) *Das Assoziationsexperiment in der therapeutischen Praxis*, Fellbach: Bonz.

Kast, V. (1992) *The Dynamics of Symbols*, New York: Fromm International.

Kaufman, G. (1989) *The Psychology of Shame*, New York: Springer.

Kernberg, O. F. (1975) *Borderline Conditions and Pathological Narcissism*, New York: Aronson.

Kielholz, P. (1967) *Angst: Psychische und somatische Aspekte*, Bern and Stuttgart: Huber.

Der Kleine Pauly (1979) *Lexikon der Antike*, München: Deutscher Taschenbuchverlag.

Köhler, L. (1988) "Neuere Forschungsergebnisse auf dem Gebiet der Kleinkindforschung," seminar held in Zürich in Nov. 1988.

Kohut, H. (1971a) *The Analysis of the Self*, New York: International Universities Press.

Kohut, H. (1971b) "Thoughts on Narcissism and Narcissistic Rage," in Ornstein, P. H. (ed.) (1980) *Selected Writings of Heinz Kohut*, vol. 2, New York: International Universities Press.

Kohut, H. (1977) *The Restoration of the Self*, New York: International Universities Press.

Krafft-Ebing, R. (1892) "Bemerkungen über 'geschlechtliche Hörigkeit' und Masochismus," *Jahrbücher für Psychiatrie* 10: 199–211.

Lewis, H. B. (1971) *Shame and Guilt in Neurosis*, New York: International Universities Press.

Lewis, H. B. (1987a) "Shame and the Narcissistic Personality," in Nathanson, D. L. (ed.) *The Many Faces of Shame*, pp. 93–132, New York and London: Guilford Press.

Lewis, H. B. (ed.) (1987b) *The Role of Shame in Symptom Formation*, Hillsdale, N. J. and London: Lawrence Erlbaum.

BIBLIOGRAPHY

Lynd, H. M. (1961) *On Shame and the Search for Identity*, New York: Science Editions.
Mahler, M. S., Pine, F. and Bergman, A. (1975) *The Psychological Birth of the Human Infant*, New York: Basic Books.
Mattern-Ames, E. (1987) *Notes on Early Damage and Regression*, Diploma Thesis, C. G. Jung Institute, Zürich.
Miller, S. (1985) *The Shame Experience*, Hillsdale, N. J. and London: Lawrence Erlbaum.
Moser, T. (1984) *Kompass der Seele*, Frankfurt a. M.: Suhrkamp.
Nathanson, D. L. (1987a) "A Timetable for Shame," in Nathanson, D. L. (ed.) *The Many Faces of Shame*, pp. 1–63, New York and London: Guilford Press.
Nathanson, D. L. (ed.) (1987b) *The Many Faces of Shame*, New York and London: Guilford Press.
Neumann, E. (1954) "On the Moon and Matriarchal Consciousness," in Berry, P. (ed.) (1990) *Fathers and Mothers*, pp. 210–30, Dallas: Spring Publications.
Neumann, E. (1955) *The Great Mother*, London: Routledge & Kegan Paul.
Neumann, E. (1962) *Origins and History of Consciousness*, London: Routledge & Kegan Paul.
Neumann, E. (1988) *The Child*, London: Karnac.
Parin, P., Morgenthaler, F. and Parin-Matthey, G. (1971) *Fürchte deinen Nächsten wie dich selbst*, Frankfurt a.M.: Suhrkamp.
Portmann, A. (1958) *Zoologie und das neue Bild des Menschen*, Hamburg: Rowholt.
Qualls-Corbett, N. (1988) *The Sacred Prostitute*, Toronto: Inner City Books.
Redfearn, J. W. T. (1985) *My Self, My Many Selves*, London: Academic Press.
Rohde-Dachser, Ch. (1989) "Abschied von der Schuld der Mütter," *Praxis der Psychotherapie und Psychosomatik* 34 (5): 250–60. Berlin: Springer.
Rousseau, J.-J. (1926) *Rousseau's Emile or Treatise on Education*, New York and London: Appleton.
Rousseau, J.-J. (1954) *The Confessions of Jean-Jacques Rousseau*, Harmondsworth: Penguin Books.
Samuels, A. (1989) "Analysis and Pluralism: the Politics of Psyche," *Journal of Analytical Psychology* 34 (1): 33–51. London: Academic Press.
Sander, L. W. (1983) "To Begin with – Reflections on Ontogeny," in Lichtenberg, J. and Kaplan, S. (eds) *Reflections on Self Psychology*, pp. 85–104, Hillsdale, N.J.: Analytic Press.
Schmidbauer, W. (1977) *Die hilflosen Helfer*, Reinbek bei Hamburg: Rowohlt.
Schneider, K. (1959) *Klinische Psychopathologie*, Stuttgart:Thieme.
Segal, H. (1964) *Introduction to the Work of Melanie Klein*, London: Hogarth Press.
Sidoli, M. (1988) "Shame and the Shadow," *Journal of Analytical Psychology* 33 (2): 127–42. London: Academic Press.
Spiegelman, J. M. (1989) "The One and the Many: Jung and the Post-Jungians," *Journal of Analytical Psychology*, 34 (1): 53–71. London: Academic Press.
Spitz, R. A. (1965) *The First Year of Life*, New York: International Universities Press.
Stern, D. N. (1985) *The Interpersonal World of the Infant*, New York: Basic Books.
Tobel, R. von (1945) *Pablo Casals*, Erlenbach-Zürich: Rotapfel-Verlag.
Tomkins, S. S. (1963) *Affect, Imagery, Consciousness, 2: The Negative Affects*, New York: Springer.
Tomkins, S. S. (1987) "Shame," in Nathanson, D. L. (ed.) *The Many Faces of Shame*, pp. 133–61, New York and London: Guilford Press.
Webster's Third New International Dictionary of the English Language (1990), Springfield, MA: Merriam.
Wharton, B. (1990) "The Hidden Face of Shame: the Shadow, Shame and Separation," *Journal of Analytical Psychology* 35 (3): 279–99. London: Routledge.
Wickler, W. (1973) "Die ethologische Deutung einiger Wächterfiguren auf Bali," in

Eibl-Eibesfeld, I. (ed.) *Der vorprogrammierte Mensch*, pp. 248–56. Vienna: Molden.

Winnicott, D. W. (1958) "The Capacity to be Alone," in *The Maturational Processes and the Facilitating Environment*, pp. 29–36, London: Hogarth Press, reprinted London: Karnac Books, 1990.

Winnicott, D. W. (1960) "Ego Distortion in Terms of True and False Self," in *The Maturational Processes and the Facilitating Environment*, pp. 140–52, London: Hogarth Press, reprinted London: Karnac Books, 1990.

Winnicott, D. W. (1963) "The Development of the Capacity for Concern," in *The Maturational Processes and the Facilitating Environment*, pp. 73–82, London: Hogarth Press, reprinted London: Karnac Books, 1990.

Winnicott, D. W. (1965) *The Maturational Processes and the Facilitating Environment*, London: Hogarth Press, reprinted London: Karnac Books, 1990.

Wirtz, U. (1989) *Seelenmord*, Zürich: Kreuz Verlag.

Wurmser, L. (1981) *The Mask of Shame*, Baltimore and London: Johns Hopkins University Press.

Wurmser, L. (1988) "Gedanken zur Psychopathologie von Scham und Ressentiment," *Analytische Psychologie* 19 (4): 283–306. Basle: Karger.

Zimmer, H. (1938) *Weisheit Indiens*, Darmstadt: Wittich.

INDEX

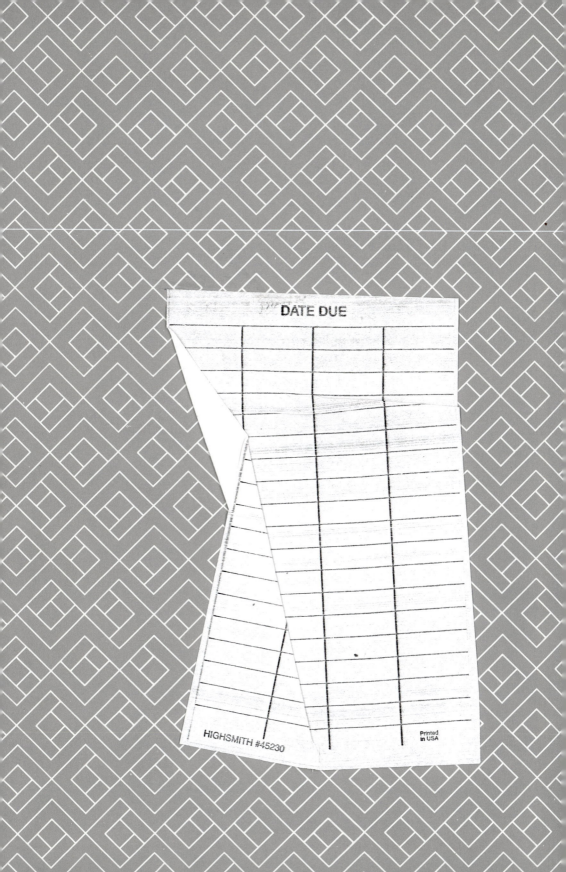

DATE DUE

HIGHSMITH #45230

Printed
in USA